The Autobiographical Demand of Place

Complicated Conversation

A Book Series of Curriculum Studies

William F. Pinar
General Editor

Vol. 21

PETER LANG
New York • Washington, D.C./Baltimore • Bern
Frankfurt am Main • Berlin • Brussels • Vienna • Oxford

Brian Casemore

The Autobiographical Demand of Place

Curriculum Inquiry in the American South

PETER LANG
New York • Washington, D.C./Baltimore • Bern
Frankfurt am Main • Berlin • Brussels • Vienna • Oxford

Library of Congress Cataloging-in-Publication Data

Casemore, Brian.
The autobiographical demand of place: curriculum inquiry
in the American south / Brian Casemore.
p. cm. — (Complicated conversation; v. 21)
Includes bibliographical references and index.
1. Curriculum planning—Philosophy. 2. Education—Curricula— Philosophy.
3. Autobiography—Authorship. 4. Critical pedagogy. I. Title.
LB2806.15.C374 375.0001—dc22 2007013526
ISBN 978-0-8204-8805-9
ISSN 1534-2816

Bibliographic information published by **Die Deutsche Bibliothek**.
Die Deutsche Bibliothek lists this publication in the "Deutsche
Nationalbibliografie"; detailed bibliographic data is available
on the Internet at http://dnb.ddb.de/.

Cover image *Red Bud/F150,* Baton Rouge, courtesy of Michael Book
Cover design by Joni Holst

29 Broadway, 18th floor, New York, NY 10006
www.peterlang.com

CONTENTS

FOREWORD

Brian and I met coincidentally, reminding us of both the capriciousness of lived experience and its "free associational" nature. We met in a study group on psychoanalysis held at George Washington University, where Brian teaches in the Education Department and where I had taught in the English Department for many years. This in itself is not extraordinary; it happens every day. But it became more auspicious for us to discover that we lived practically next door to one another, in yet another part of the city, in carriage house residences that face out into a covert, and frankly trash-heaped, alley, and from which neither one of us has access to the main street. We were neighbors, sharing some of the same vegetation and bird and floral life; in fact, it had been the dejected stance of the sunflowers in Brian's own front yard that had moved me to write a poem about endurance; it was the silver birch that greeted him every day on which I had noted a squirrel's nest in the shape of a saint's head. Now that I'd met Brian, these personal notations of mine had a link with an *actual* person, and that person was sitting next to me in a seminar that had nothing to do with my solo morning walks or reveries. A roaming signifier or set of signifiers found a new *inter*personal context for expression, enriching its meaning, making it more social and valuable. We had, in a word, expanded our mutual boundaries to include the nesting of the other.

So the next time I saw a robin perch on the edge of a roof gutter or, more acrobatically, on the head of a chrysanthemum, I knew that the same bird could be passing in Brian's purview, and that his thoughts were linked to mine in a way that only the unconscious, in its free-floating, serendipitous way, could register. What I didn't know then, but know now, is that Brian had written a book that had surpassed my own study of painful literature, one that would broaden our understanding not only of Southern place specifically but also of the psychological trends that make testimony necessary. Such a book would have to take risks while offering a more balanced view of our national history.

America needs a witness. And in this ambitious new book, Brian is just that, as he considers Southern place from a range of theoretical perspectives, demonstrating how the recognizable definition of place is contingent on certain identifications we make with our cultural surroundings. More significant is the exactitude of methodology behind Brian's research for this book. He shows how Southern literature and Southern white masculine identity are inextricably bound together, and thus reveals how the landscape compensates for a fundamental insufficiency, which may be clarified by the notion of the Lacanian "lack." With this linkage made, the author weaves a dazzling analysis of representation and desire; remembering and forgetting; and showing how the ever present-ness of irremediable loss taxes every part of our collective experience as individuals and as a culture. His close readings of Southern texts authored by some of the best African Americans writers writing today, such as Randall Kenan and Reginald McKnight, are almost as riveting as the stories themselves. His reading of Yusef Komunyakaa, an enormously influential poet, is particularly lucid and perspicacious.

Although it would seem that this project alone would be a major contribution to the field of Southern studies, Brian goes further, urging us to apply theory to praxis, and to reframe the English curriculum. Indeed, learning often means negotiation with what Deborah Britzman refers to as "difficult knowledge" in order for educators to impart the principles of social justice to their students effectively. In a bold attempt to do just that, Brian undertakes the task of self-analysis, examining his own associations and preconceptions about place in order to correct and revise them. To his own life he applies his own theories, as if to test their veracity. Intriguingly, he interweaves the autobiographical with the theoretical through what he terms "interludes," which trace the dimensions of introspection and image making about the landscape simultaneously.

Thus, in pursuit of difficult knowledge, Brian's study works to deconstruct public assumptions about Southernness and to point the way to authentic self-realization, working through (in the Freudian reparative sense) to social transformation. In keeping with his mentor, William Pinar, the author suggests a more flexible and self-revelatory practice of learning for teachers and students, including the use of autobiographical writing and discovery. And, by honoring the immediacy and complexity of his students, Brian joins a number of psychoanalytic and pedagogical theorists, and Southern studies scholars, including Jeffrey Berman and Mark Bracher, Patricia Yaeger, Ellen Douglas, and even the poet Dave Smith, in elucidating classroom culture and its potential to shape national culture. He offers us hope. But most important, in allowing himself to exercise his personal voice, and to be present in the text, Brian creates a cultural and pedagogical study that is not only transformative but also beautifully, and powerfully, crafted.

Judith Harris

ACKNOWLEDGMENTS

Many people generously supported me as I conducted this research. I am deeply grateful for their counsel, encouragement, and love. My teachers in particular provided invaluable intellectual and personal guidance. I thank Flo Durway for her inspiring invitation into the world of teaching, Paula Salvio for her trust in my voice and writing, and Elsie Michie for her continual effort to move me toward new insight. I want to thank Bill Doll for his unceasing support of my teaching and research and Claudia Eppert for inviting me to explore autobiography as a collaborative process.

My deepest gratitude goes to Bill Pinar for his extremely generous teaching and guidance. With great patience, Bill taught me the importance of allowing my intellectual concerns to emerge from and take root in my inner life. With his support, my intellectual journey into Southern place became, more deeply, a journey of the self. Bill's encouragement to "voyage out" has helped me discover many new worlds.

My family has continually inspired my thinking and desire to learn. Our relationships are at the foundation of this project. My parents, Jackie and Gary, have given me abundant care and support. By their example, I have learned to question the world, to challenge my own thinking, and to listen to the experience of others. I want to thank them above all for creating a home that fostered capaciousness of thought. For speaking to me through their passion for life, literature, art, and music, I thank my sister and brother, Julie and Mark. They have been my most imaginative and daring teachers. I want to thank my sister-in-law, Kristin, whose love of language endlessly enlivens my own. And I thank my uncle Louis Lowrey for helping me find spirit in the pursuit of social justice.

Many friends helped me accomplish this project. I want to express my gratitude to all of them for their intellectual and emotional support. For countless rich and exciting conversations that informed my writing, I especially want to thank Nichole Guillory, Ugena Whitlock, Jen Gilbert, Nolde Alexius, and Alice Ann Fesmire.

During the final stages of this project, Katayoon Majd was a vital source of encouragement and support. She provided valuable perspective, care, and conversation as I began my life in Washington, DC. And she continues to help me articulate and understand the emerging sense of place I feel in my new home. For Katayoon's love and friendship, I am deeply grateful.

Judith Harris inspired my thought at a critical time in the writing of this book. Through her poetry, literary criticism, autobiographical writing, and, most important, our daily conversations, Judith pulled the veil from the mystery of the writing process, reminding me that writing can indeed sustain a life. I will leave the story of our remarkable meeting for Judith to tell, which she does in the Foreword. Here I want to thank her for sharing her gifts as a teacher, thinker, poet, and friend. Judith has a gift for introducing people to the unmarked, the unseen, and the half-spoken parts of life in such a way that inspires subtle movement and deep understanding of one's inner world. I know no one who uses this gift so ethically and brilliantly as she does.

Many years ago, long before I began this project, Claesi Cashio imagined I would write a book, supposing that it would take a book to capture all the thoughts that I tried in my late teens so anxiously and excitedly to communicate. Since then, I have often relied on Claesi's prediction as support for my writing process, using her imagined book to contain the tumult of my writing life. While completing this project, I came to think of her prediction as an expression of faith in the difficult work of growing up. This book is dedicated to Claesi, as promised.

INTRODUCTION

The Question of Southern Place in an Autobiographical Curriculum

We take our measure of being from what surrounds us, and what surrounds us is always, to some extent, of our own making.

—Robert Pogue Harrison (2002, p. 349)

Where are we moored? What / are the bindings? What be- / hooves us?

—Adrienne Rich (1991, p. 12)

I want to understand the role of place in my experience. As a figure of autobiographical inquiry, place signifies the diverse and intersecting worlds in which I dwell, to which I contribute meaning, and from which I take the measure of my being. Place indicates particular contexts in which I am immersed as well as my subjective interaction with these private, social, and aesthetic spaces. In my encounter with the particularities of place, an elusive past and an ambiguous future coalesce. Through place, I question the relationship between the object world and my internal landscape, the public sphere and the localities of my internal life. My experience of place thus bears the history of the way I have been called into various forms of culture and community and can reveal possibilities for my continual reengagement with a complex social world.

My intellectual interest in place emerges from my study of the American South and my effort to conceptualize a Southern curriculum dedicated to social justice—a curriculum that takes account of the autobiographical roots of knowledge and society using the interpretive tools of psychoanalysis. Place is central to such a curriculum. It is a fundamental trope in regional self-identification, and the question of the significance of place pervades Southern literature and criticism. When teaching in the region, therefore, I turn to the topic of place to help my students—future educators—envision the social and political environment we create together. The heightened significance of place in Southern studies and regional culture invites us to interrogate the meaning and function of this environment in our everyday lives.

When theorized in its complexity, the concept of place complicates our autobiographies and can unsettle our taken-for-granted views of the world. In the South, however, "place" is bound up with platitudes of white patriarchal culture, in particular with the "sense of place" assumed to be a fundamental trait of authentic Southern identity. Traditionally, for the white South, as demonstrated in the writing of Donald Davidson and Ellen Douglas, place represents the determinative ground of the social order, and the ground to which an idyllic fantasy of Southern community is tied. The endlessly affirmed "sense of place" endows the fantasy with the status of reality in the eyes of white Southerners. In its most rigid form, this cultural rhetoric demands the adherence of individuals to dominant cultural values and excludes questions of conflict and dissent from the public sphere (Romine, 2002).

To unsettle this cultural rhetoric, Scott Romine (2002) suggests we approach "place" not only as a setting in a literary place, or a physical landscape to which an author alludes, but also as a text that demands reading as a cultural practice. In other words, rather than locating and defining place *in* the South or *in* Southern literature, we might ask, What does a particular discourse of place accomplish? What codes and norms does it establish? What identities, perspectives, and ways of knowing does it include and exclude? What does it defend and abject?

In this vein, several contemporary Southern critics (Romine, 1999, 2002; Smith, 2002; Yaeger, 2000) review the dominant discourse of place in Southern literature to show how a highly cathected though seemingly innocuous conception of place obscures the region's history and politics. Place gratifies a wish for a paradisiacal past. In the texts I will be discussing, the narcissistic identification with mastery over the land provides a medium for the unconscious gratification of racist impulses. I want to emphasize this point. To investigate "place" in the South is to take up a discourse that has been used to obscure conditions of domination and oppression and to prevent political resistance and social change. Southern place has achieved mythic status, exemplified in William Faulkner's and Eudora Welty's fiction. Were it not for its loaded meanings, place could not command this kind of reverence and desire. It is a topic, therefore, worthy of much scholarly attention.

Romine (1999) reveals this problem of mixed meanings as he examines writers of the Southern conservative tradition. In *The Narrative Forms of Southern Community,* he argues the white South's reductive conception of place found its most shrewd supporter in Donald Davidson. Davidson imagined the Southern writer's relationship to place in terms of an "autochthonous ideal," arguing the "authentic" Southern writer should remain under the sway of his natural environment without protesting or explaining the social order. Through this notion, Davidson "advocated that the southern writer *dwell in* . . . the tacit dimension of his culture rather than focusing on it from a perspective from which it might appear quaint, backward, or ideologically deviant" (p. 11). The autochthonous ideal thus represents a model of subjectivity as it relates to place, one that values compliance with the status quo. As we will learn, Davidson's conception of place was rooted in his reactionary racial politics. And his ideas generally have been a significant influence on American conservative thought (Murphy, 2001). But the notion that the value of Southern place is innate and self-evident finds its way into moderate and progressive conversations about the South, infusing them with a reactionary view of Southern culture and society.

In *Dirt and Desire: Reconstructing Southern Women's Writing, 1930–1990,* Patricia Yaeger (2000) suggests that this attachment to the traditional conception of place hinges on a romantic belief that place endows life with unquestionable meaning and coherence. Despite the racial antagonism and social upheaval that have defined the region, this romantic belief survives in Southern truisms about place. Many Southerners hold to the axiom that "place does endow" (Welty quoted in Yaeger, 2000, p. 23). Left unquestioned, this phrase of Eudora Welty's, Yaeger argues, leads to a "vision of place associated with romanticism [and] the virtues of rootedness," and therefore obscures or "blocks" conditions of social conflict (p. 14). For example, Southern critics defend Welty's maxim with the argument that Southerners across the racial divide are "caught up in writing out of and redefining the meaning of place" (p. 23). However, rather than disclosing the antagonism and injustice that entangle both black and white writers in the foundations of the region, many critics claim this cultural diversity confirms that Southern place is inherent to the benign capacities and experiences of Southerners. The question of place, if continually raised, simply leads back to claims that

> [w]e in the South have grown up being narrators. We have lived in a place—that's the word, Place—where storytelling is a way of life. . . . Our concept of place isn't just history or philosophy; it's a sensory thing of sights and smells and seasons and earth and water and sky as well. (Welty quoted in Yaeger, 2000, p. 13)

In many treatments of Southern place, claims to a predilection for storytelling and a heightened experience of the natural environment mask palpable social and historical tensions. However, in her analysis of Southern women's writing, Yaeger does not flinch from identifying what makes Southern place such a palpable presence. "If place is so weighty and important in twentieth-century southern literature," she writes, "it is because its central figure (even after the sixties) is so constant. It is, and remains, the specter of segregation" (p. 23). Exploding the traditional, romanticized conception of Southern place, Yaeger argues that "place is never simply 'place' in Southern writing, but always a site where trauma has been absorbed into the landscape" (p. 13).

In this present study of Southern place, I will foreground the conditions of racial injustice in the region. This will remind us how the region's traumatic racial history subtends seemingly innocent feelings of belonging to the South. As I explore the traditional conception of Southern place, I will also analyze it in terms of gender. Yaeger (2000) again leads the way.

Through her incisive and daring review of Southern women's writing, Yaeger (2000) constructs new categories for the analysis of Southern literature and culture. Yaeger "dynamites the rails" of the Southern literary tradition that has secured the canonical status of white male writers. She does so by turning to the "black and white women writers who felt at home within yet deeply estranged from the South of the twentieth century," women writers with a "fierceness" and "power," a "flagrant desire to abuse a form of cultural capital not traditionally their own" (p. 2). This treatment of Southern women's writing, then, opens up "alternative phenomenologies of place" that help remap the South as social and subjective terrain (p. 22).

Inspired by Yaeger's gender analysis, I return to the traditional conception of Southern place to reveal aspects of white masculinity it leaves unquestioned. In my gender analysis, I want to reveal the way Southern place has functioned as a projection and protective harbor for beleaguered white masculinity. With this perspective on place, I will be able to expose the distance between the lived experience of white male identity and its hegemonic ideal (DiPiero, 2002). This exposure, finally, will lead to my affirmation of white male subjectivity lived at the margins of Southern culture. The work of Kaja Silverman (1992) provides the theoretical framework for this analysis.

The romanticized vision of Southern place can be read in terms of the "dominant fiction," a concept Silverman (1992) develops in her study of masculinities that refuse phallic authority. Though Romine (1999, 2002) emphasizes the racialized character of the traditional conception of Southern place and Yaeger (2000) highlights the women's perspectives it obscures, the dominant fiction can help expose its entanglement with conventional white masculinity.

In *Male Subjectivity at the Margins,* Silverman (1992) describes the way human subjects inhabit and accept ideological fantasy as "reality." The dominant fiction refers to the ideological fantasy that commands collective belief in the adequacy of the male subject, the unity of the Oedipal family, and the coherence of the patriarchal world. Providing individuals with a sense of a proper, even if disparaged, position within the social network, the dominant fiction also solicits faith in its validity by providing the space for the collective affirmation of social norms. Silverman's theory is, therefore, well suited to the project of exposing a romanticized conception of place. She explains that this ideological network "provides each subject with more than an image of 'self.' It also depicts the surrounding environment, the *vraisemblance* which the . . . subject inhabits" (p. 24). Moreover, she asserts, "[this] ideology constitutes not only the subject, but the world" (p. 24).

Yaeger (2000) argues "we need to contemplate both the *phenomenologies* of place that bind texts together and the multiregional facts and perspectives on place that change from decade to decade and blow texts apart" (p. 23). This argument has encouraged me to look again at my own experience of place, and, with insights from a range of disciplines, to read *into* Southern place the gendered and racialized conflicts that are inherent in a region with a legacy of slavery. In this book, therefore, I attempt to shatter the belief in the white male Southerner's autochthonous and harmonious relationship to Southern place. By taking up a fundamental trope in Southern studies, I hope to demonstrate a process of working through a cultural symptom, a process that can contribute to the progressive reconstruction of the American South.

A Curriculum of Place in the American South

This research explores the language of Southern place as it is represented in the voices and perspectives of writers who are variously bound by the region, its history, and its myths. It promotes understanding of the educational experience of confronting and working through one's relationship to the history and politics of the American South, and it emphasizes the way this experience is expressed in terms of place. The study is grounded in autobiographical inquiry, which appears as personal narrative and social-psychoanalytic self-reflection throughout the book. Southern texts—literature and criticism from and about the American South—guide the research, providing insight into subjective encounters with Southern history, place, and politics and illuminating the process and problems of articulating the educational experience such encounters afford.

My work contributes to curriculum theory by investigating educational experience in autobiographical and sociopolitical context. More specifically, it follows writers in the field who theorize a curriculum of place in the American South (Kincheloe & Pinar, 1991; Slattery & Daigle, 1994; Pinar, 2004). In my contribution to this conversation, I emphasize that "place" not only refers to a location or region but also absorbs subjective meanings and social identities. This emphasis allows me to analyze the way the traditional conception of Southern place supports hegemonic white masculinity. And it helps me theorize the process of working through "place" as a cultural symptom.

Toward these ends, I both interpret elements of a Southern curriculum as manifested in literary and historical texts and attempt to construct a Southern curriculum that fosters the analysis of subjectivity and social identity. With my exploration of the language of place in the South, I want to show how texts resonate from within, marking the socialized region and its history. My inquiry is thus interdisciplinary and autobiographical. It draws on psychoanalysis, Southern studies, and the philosophy of place—as well as on theories of curriculum, literature, and art.

The following questions underlie my inquiry. What is the role of place in self-formation? How does a conception of place mediate our relationship to society and history? What does our understanding of place suggest about our subjective and social identities? What is the relationship between white male identity and the dominant discourse of Southern place? How do autobiographical investigations of Southern place risk complying with the status quo? How might they reveal paths to social change?

Working within a tradition of autobiographical research in the field of curriculum theory (see Pinar, Reynolds, Slattery, & Taubman, 1995, pp. 515–566), I represent my personal concerns in autobiographical narratives and explore them, indirectly, through the analysis of literary and critical texts. The concept of *currere*, theorized by Pinar and Grumet (1976) in *Toward a Poor Curriculum,* informs my understanding of this autobiographical curriculum research. *Currere* refers to the subjective experience of social, cultural, and institutional structures and the process of rendering that experience for further inquiry. My research specifically draws on the psychoanalytic foundations of *currere*. In *Understanding Curriculum,* Pinar et al. (1995) explain that in terms of psychoanalysis, *currere* "involves the examination of manifest and latent meaning, conscious and unconscious content of language, as well as the political implications of such reflection and interpretation" (p. 521). Language, the theory of *currere* teaches, is never free of the outside influences and secondary meanings culture has imposed upon it. Its rhetorical intricacies, then, come with a cost, often obscuring deeper narratives of injustice and civil strife. If we accept that place is ideological as well as physically dimensional, created in the mind and through language as well as the landscape, and thus constituted through certain values, some prejudicial, we have an opportunity to explore it as something that emerges laden with personal and public meanings. But first we must unsettle it.

The Significance of Place: An Interdisciplinary Review

> *As places animate the ideas and feelings of persons who attend to them, these same ideas and feelings animate the places on which attention has been bestowed.*
>
> —Keith Basso (1996, p. 55)

> *I've always felt that the creative impulse comes from a need to hold onto a place in time.*
>
> —Nolde Alexius (2004, p. 61)

> *What was here is inseparable from what is here.*
>
> —Lucy Lippard (1997, p. 116)

In *The Lure of the Local: Senses of Place in a Multicentered Society,* art critic Lucy Lippard (1997) investigates the politics and power of place at the intersection of social history, lived experience, and contemporary art. Exploring "historical narrative as it is written *in* the landscape or place by the people who live or lived there," Lippard uncovers "the pull of place that operates on each of us, exposing our politics and spiritual legacies" (p. 7). For Lippard this draw toward the history and meaning of place "is the geographical component of the psychological need to belong somewhere, one antidote to a prevailing alienation" (p. 7). Lippard is concerned with the way this lure into a deepened relationship with place is both honored and ignored, both creatively undertaken and fearfully disavowed.

As she works through this tension, her theorization of place suggests a route into social-psychoanalytic inquiry. "The lure of the local," she writes, "is that undertone to modern life that connects it to the past we know so little and the future we are aimlessly concocting" (p. 7). Lippard gives social and historical weight to our singular and often elusive experiences of place. She thus challenges us to question how, through a desire to grasp the meaning of place, we might transform a tenuous relationship to history into a substantial interweaving of historical and life narratives.

The tenuousness of the connection between modern life and the past, Pierre Nora (1989) argues, can be explained through history's destruction of memory. Nora differentiates history, a representation of the past that arrogates universal authority, and memory, a lived phenomenon "open to the dialectic of remembering and forgetting" (p. 8). History dictates a constant progression of time, claiming to represent an unadulterated past, thus depleting the past of its lived character. Memory, on the other hand, fluctuates and evolves with the vicissitudes of lived experience, as it emerges spontaneously from individual and collective encounters with the world. The result of this difference and the nearly ubiquitous investment in "unself-conscious, commanding, all-powerful" history is the loss of the capacity "to live *within* memory" (p. 8, my emphasis).

Memory and place, Nora (1989) suggests, are fundamentally entwined. He reveals the function of place in his conception of memory, explaining how "history binds itself strictly to temporal continuities" whereas "memory takes root in the concrete, in spaces, gestures, images, and objects" (p. 9). Further revealing the connection between place and memory, Nora explains that the loss of "real environments of memory" necessitates the experience of and an often-anxious search for "lieux de mémoire" or "sites of memory" (p. 7). Conceptualizing the significance of such sites, Nora ultimately shows that the loss of lived memory to dictatorial history is felt in terms of place. He writes: "[C]onsciousness of the break with the past is bound up with the sense that memory has been torn—but torn in such a way as to pose the problem of the embodiment of memory in certain sites where a sense of historical continuity persists" (p. 7).

The modern investment in objective and authoritative time thus diminishes not only memory but also our conception and experience of place. Edward Casey (1993) makes this argument convincingly in *Getting Back into Place:*

> If we construe world-order as time-order, then the world, including our own world, is at all times in imminent demise. . . . No sooner does an event occur *in* time than it goes *out of* time. . . . The crux of the problem is that time is conceived in such a way that

> everything else is made subjacent to it, beginning with place and ending with space. (pp. 7–10)

With time understood as chronology and history given a dominant authority, we lose at a rapid pace not only the lived memory but also the place significance of our experiences, experiences constantly escaping into an irretrievable, spatialized past.

Together Lippard, Casey, and Nora reveal the consequences of severing lived and embodied relationships to the past. The loss of memory troubles the intimate connection between place and subjectivity. If the place-world holds memory, then, in the modern context of a nearly eradicated memory, returning to place, exploring the significance of place, should begin to disclose what is lost. Lippard's (1997) earlier point applies: The lure of the local connects us to the past we have forgotten. The question then becomes, How will we negotiate what a return to place brings about, that is, the exposure of "our politics and spiritual legacies" (p. 7)? How, in other words, do we confront and work through the aspects of ourselves and our relations to others that have been obscured in our experiences of place?

In *Psychoanalysis and the Scene of Reading,* Mary Jacobus (1999) shows how literary landscapes (landscapes depicted in fiction) signify psychical dynamics, specifically negotiations with loss, absence, and otherness. She writes,

> Looking at landscape involves ideas about absence and distance, and can even imply looking away. In this sense, landscape is less what we see in our mind's eye than what we don't see—our peculiar, unconscious way of relating to an inner world (p. 54).

By resuscitating the significance of place in literary criticism and revealing the dynamic function of place within narrative, Jacobus characterizes reading as the (re)negotiation of an internal landscape. In her formulation, literary landscapes frequently represent (through a negation) conditions of troubled object relations and experiences of loss. Jacobus explains: "[T]he landscape of absence typically functions to deny or make bearable spacial [*sic*] or temporal breaks between persons, or even within ourselves." Landscape images may obscure or simply mollify an awareness of breached relations, but they may also serve as a medium of communication with what is lost; that is, they may serve as a site for working through personal and historical trauma. The landscape of absence, Jacobus continues, "can equally be a way to maintain connection or preserve memory—a way to think. *Not* being there can be as important as being there; what has gone may be as significant as what remains" (p. 55, emphasis in original).

Jacobus's (1999) theory of literary landscapes informs my study of place in Southern texts and social-psychoanalytic curricula. For Jacobus, landscapes represent forms of subjectivity, serve as psychical links in the face of subjective fragmentation, and maintain the relevance of what is lost, forgotten, and uncertain. This conceptualization of landscape revivifies the power of place in subjective experience. Moreover it can heighten our awareness of exclusions in our perceptions of place, a process of awakening necessary for any rigorous study of the American South. Questioning landscapes familiar and strange to us, those we cathect in pleasure and aversion, can lead us to personal and historical narratives that are obscured in our experiences of place.

W. J. T. Mitchell (2002a) provides another psychoanalytic approach to place. In his preface to the second edition of *Landscape and Power,* Mitchell discusses place in terms of Lacanian theory. Lacan's theory of the subject is amenable to this interpretation because it defines subjectivity as a place in language, an imaginary place that has no real physical dimensions, but is the representation of a place as mimeticized in the mind. This place in language—"the place from which we speak" (Žižek, 1989, p. 155)—occurs at the intersection of three registers: the Imaginary, the Symbolic, and the Real. These registers ensure the constant unfolding of subjectivity rather than the presence of being. That is, though the subject is a place or position in language, language cannot represent the totality of the subject. In the register of the Imaginary, the subject achieves a semblance of totality, but the subject is constitutively divided (self-alienated) by the Symbolic Other, which is the unconscious or significatory excess of language. As Tim Dean (1991) explains, "the subject is 'split' by language, inaugurally alienated, and thus 'on trial' in the sense of having constantly to try and legitimate itself by finding a stable, habitable place in language" (pp. 20–21).

In this psychoanalytic framework, Mitchell (2002a) theorizes the broader notion of place, which can be applied more narrowly to "Southern place." To disrupt the binaries that reduce place to a hermetic (natural or cultural; social or subjective; secure or alienating) realm, he argues for a triadic conceptualization of place in terms of space, place, and landscape. Mitchell relates these terms to the registers Lacan theorizes (the Symbolic, the Imaginary, and the Real) and suggests that reading Lacan's Symbolic as a spatial register may further our understanding of the way "law, prohibition, regulation and control"—characteristics of the Symbolic—are encoded in landscapes (p. x). In this framework, landscapes coincide with Lacan's Imaginary; they are visual phenomena that correspond with the aggregate ego. Therefore, Mitchell suggests, we might read the social codes of space in our visual perceptions of landscape, the law in the visual register where we seek a secure and unified sense of self. Completing the triad, Mitchell puts forth "the notion of place as the location of the Lacanian Real" (p. x). In Lacanian psychoanalysis, the Real refers to bodily states and affects that exceed both our capacity to make meaning in language and the sense of self-coherence we gain through the visual perception of our surroundings. As a vector of the Real, then, "place" signifies something ineffable, "the site of trauma or the historical event" (pp. x–xi).

Reading the broad notion of place through Lacanian theory, Mitchell (2002a) argues, can reveal "the way an imaginary landscape is woven into the fabric of real places . . . and symbolic spaces" (p. xi). This analysis disallows a strict boundary between interiority and exteriority and, therefore, can help expose the inevitable transference that accompanies our treatments of place. Transference, which is central to the psychoanalytic process, can illuminate the way the unconscious informs the construction of place and place-based communities.

Another essay in *Landscape and Power* posits human subjectivity as fundamental to the meaning of place, setting the foreground for the topic at hand. Robert Pogue Harrison (2002) argues places do not preexist human contact but rather "come into being through acts of human grounding" (p. 350). As we investigate the meaning of place, he points out, we continually find ourselves in the tension between literal and subjective ground. Harrison explores this tension. In doing so, he traces the human signs by which places come into being to the institution of burial. The ground on which a place rests binds us (the living and the dead) through our mortality. Reminding us we are all latecomers to the places in which we dwell, Harrison argues that human subjectivity is fundamentally "preinhabited by those who came before" (p. 353).

Following Mitchell (2002a) and Harrison (2002), I understand places to be created through human signification. They are products of our signifying the "here" of experience (Harrison, 2002, p. 350). With these writers, I also understand human signification to be ineluctably transpersonal. However private and personal our language, it reaches beyond individuality into a social realm, seeking a response from an Other. As subjects of place, therefore, we endlessly position ourselves within a social sphere as we contribute to the construction of this shared world.

The worlds we inhabit are shared worlds. Being-in-place is being with others (Casey, 1996; Richardson, 2002). This fact gives me cause to investigate the relationship and tension between my subjective experience of place and the social, cultural, and historical conditions of the places I inhabit. But what determines my singular sense of place? How do the broader conditions and practices of place inform my being uniquely "thrown" into the world?[1] And how can I attend to this intermediate region of experience, where the self expands and subjectivity intermingles with a complex social sphere?

Joe Kincheloe and William Pinar (1991) illuminate the educational value and political potential of such inquiries into place. In their edited collection *Curriculum As Social Psychoanalysis: The Significance of Place,* they argue place is "an important means of linking particularity to the social concerns of curriculum theory" (p. 21). This is the crux of the problem of place in the American South. Though there is arguably a heightened phenomenological and conceptual relationship to place in the region, and thus an increased potential for linking particularity to social concerns, place-particular knowledge has historically fuelled the region's conservative localism and anti-intellectualism. In the white, male-dominated South, a focus on the particularity of place has, in part, promoted "isolation from the insight of more general analytical devices" (p. 14). Situating their study of place in the American South, Kincheloe and Pinar explain that "[t]he southern fury against social theoretical generalization that emerges from a radical particularity often encourages an idea-related xenophobia, a discomfort with the intellectual, an aversion to analysis, and a reluctance to embrace reform and social change" (p. 14). The study of place in the American South, these writers make clear, demands a progressive social and educational project.

Kincheloe and Pinar (1991) turn to the literature of the South to recover a Southern conception of place open to social and psychoanalytic movement. The work of Eudora Welty, for instance, serves as an important example of the way autobiographical inquiry can be focused through the experience of place, how an "analyzed sense of place" can become "a vehicle to self-knowledge" (p. 6). Against romanticized interpretations of her work, Kincheloe and Pinar show that Welty values reflection on the intermingling of internal and external worlds. She writes: "[O]ur knowledge depends on the living relationship between what we see going on and ourselves" (quoted in Kincheloe & Pinar, 1991, p. 21). Thus, through her exploration of place, Welty can provide a foundation for opening the particularities of self-narrative to social, historical, and ethical insights (p. 7).

Other Southern writers help Kincheloe and Pinar (1991) articulate a conception of place that illuminates Southern history. In his essay in the collection, Pinar (1991) paraphrases Lewis Simpson's (1983) argument that "the South lost both history and memory in defending its agrarian way of life, in its denial of its status as, in Simpson's phrase, the 'garden of chattel'" (p. 175). For Pinar, however, William Faulkner's *Intruder in the Dust* brings to the fore the South's entanglement with, and need to work through, the past. Faulkner's aesthetic, that is, serves as a call to social-psychoanalytic reflection. Representing the consequences of the Civil War on the minds of Southerners, Faulkner writes: "Yesterday won't be over until tomorrow and tomorrow began ten thousand years ago" (quoted in Pinar, 1991, p. 175). Along with other Southern writers, Faulkner holds steadfastly to "the belief that the present is continually instructed by a living past" (Kincheloe & Pinar, 1991, p. 9), a belief that permeates virtually every one of his novels, particularly *The Sound and the Fury*. Following these Southern writers, Kincheloe and Pinar argue that the past must be negotiated through place, as "the loss of place precipitates the loss of history" (p. 9).

Finally, Kincheloe and Pinar (1991) highlight the Southern writer's attention to the intimacies and subtleties of place experience. In doing so, they affirm the value of an educational journey that wanders, explores depths, and tolerates uncertainty. They write,

> Southern writers find the germ of place in an often fleeting image, a particular southern shadow, the color of an aura, or an idiosyncratic detail. An overlooked particular of the southern idiom may spark a feeling for place that fashions a novel's theme, the historical monograph's interpretation, or a curriculum's focus. In other words, place builds on these shards; it collects them, juxtaposes them, and integrates them into a montage of related images. (p. 9)

Southern writers show that our subtle and intimate experiences of place contribute to the larger workings of place and region. Through our everyday means of inhabiting place, in other words, we connect to the complexities of history and the social field.

This brings us to a significant intersection of curriculum theory and the philosophy of place. Similar to the curriculum theorists Kincheloe and Pinar, Casey (1993) calls for the thorough study of place and place experience. In his analysis of the "place-world," Casey encourages us to explore the layers and vestiges of the places in our past. Borrowing Gaston Bachelard's concept of "topoanalysis," he promotes "the systematic psychological study of the localities of our intimate lives" (quoted in Casey, 1993, p. 311). Similar to Kincheloe and Pinar, Casey insists on the importance of connecting particularities of place with broader theoretical frameworks. The intellectual labor of topoanalysis, therefore, is not an invitation to "ensconce ourselves in psychical interiority." Indeed, as Casey argues, the rigorous investigation of place experience, "looks *without* as much as, and finally more than, it seeks within" (p. 312, emphasis in original).

With these writers, I am concerned with the relationship between the experience and history of place, between internal and external landscapes, and between subjectivity and the social field. In the next section, I describe the autobiographical research method I've employed in this book to disclose the meaning embedded in these relationships.

The Autobiographical Demand

My research method is one that has emerged from my pedagogy. It represents my belief in the importance of autobiographical understanding and my concern that we use autobiography in research and pedagogy to move toward and work through difficult and elusive parts of the self. Such work can increase our capacity for social and historical understanding and contribute to the process of social change.

In my teacher preparation courses, I ask my students to consider how their autobiographies conceal the lives of others. Together we ask what it means that our stories cannot be disentangled from the others we encounter. We ask what we are to do with stories that convey our sense of certainty—with stories that resonate with our most binding emotions. We ask what we are to do when we discover that our stories are rife with opacities and that they radically narrow our field of knowledge. We question where our stories seem to fail, where they trail off, and where they need silence. We ask from whom such silences might sever us.

Following these questions, our conversations sometimes wander. They often stutter and fall silent. As often, they generate significant insight. We pursue these questions to understand better the way autobiography both entangles us in and severs us from the lives of others. These questions help us attend to what is only partially spoken in our narratives. And they help us follow such traces of the self to more complex personal and cultural histories.

These questions that I bring to my teaching are informed by Leigh Gilmore's (2001) notion of an auto/biographical demand. This demand, Gilmore explains, is a force in life writing, one that joins the demands of autobiography (the call to tell my story) and the demands of biography (the call to tell *your* story). The auto/biographical demand creates "an irresolvable narrative dilemma because it both divides and doubles the writer" (p. 72). Through a disruption to the experience of self-continuity, it disseminates the question of autobiographical meaning. What intervenes in the self is the intractable story of another.

Gilmore (2001) exemplifies the auto/biographical demand with the book *Shot in the Heart,* Mikal Gilmore's account of his family history and the events surrounding the execution of his brother Gary Gilmore. As an effort to work through traumatic experiences, this narrative represents a "limit-case" of self-representation, revealing "how trauma ruptures the boundaries of the [masculine and] autonomous autobiographical 'I'" (pp. 71–72). By using this example, I do not mean to suggest that it depicts the challenges to making meaning that my students and I experience in our autobiographical investigations of otherness. It does, however, generally reveal "the demands trauma and the self make upon each other" (p. 143) and therefore opens the question of how self-representation might speak of suffering, whether one's own or another's, a question central to curricula that connect problems of self-formation with issues of social justice.

Gary Gilmore's life was thrust into public view in 1976 after he murdered two men in Utah and then petitioned the state for his execution by firing squad. Norman Mailer's *The Executioner's Song* further unfolded this story for the nation. In *Shot in the Heart,* Mikal Gilmore provides a view from within the Gilmore family's history of spectacular violence and pain. His account foregrounds the influence of Mikal and Gary's sadistic father, a man who forged his identity through abuse and deceit. Mikal Gilmore's account shows his father authoring, through physical and psychological brutality, a convoluted and incarcerating family history.

As Mikal Gilmore attempts to capture this history in writing, he encounters impenetrable secrets that disrupt the continuity of his narrative. These disjunctions call him to elaborate his complex position as both a character *within* and a spectator *of* this story of trauma. Mikal speaks to the dead. He addresses ghosts. As they disappear from view or slip from his grasp he must speak of himself, his uncertainties, and his confrontation with the void of meaning at the foundation of his personal history.

Mikal attempts to rewrite his personal history through the figure of his brother. He explores the events of his brother's psychological wounding to uncover the meaning of his own. Yet, any meaning Mikal renders autobiographically (about himself) or biographically (about his brother) is haunted by their father. The father endlessly haunts this complex fabric of transferences. Negotiating this auto/biographical demand, Mikal must contend at every turn with the father's symbolic power. With *Shot in the Heart,* therefore, Leigh Gilmore shows the auto/biographical demand to be auto/biographical transference, a site of ambivalence in the construction of meaning, where one is both drawn toward and barred from secure (self-)knowledge.

With the provocation of the auto/biographical demand, a writer faces the confusion of self-narration sliding into an account of another and description of another disclosing aspects of the self. The writing that ensues must incorporate forms and language to handle the shifting textual subject. Paula Salvio (2001) describes the effects in her work on Anne Sexton. "At the moment that I begin to tell the story of Sexton's teaching life," Salvio writes, "aspects of my life surface and demand articulation" (p. 114). She continues: "Anne Sexton appears as an uncanny interlocutor through whom I have begun to approach unresolvable questions about memory, knowledge, and the body, questions that were fused into my teaching life from the very start" (p. 103). This auto/biographical demand creates a sense of instability in her writing to which she responds with a combination of textual forms: biography, memoir, autobiography, poetry, essay, and theoretical writing (p. 114). This is a process, she explains, of approaching memory indirectly and rethinking personal and social expectations. It is a way of bringing the "autobiographical I to form in ways that can more fully contain the histories and biographies of those before us" (p. 95). Salvio thus reveals the destabilizing force of the auto/biographical demand as a place from which to begin curriculum inquiry, curriculum inquiry specifically concerned with rejuvenating marred capacities for historical understanding. Following her work, my students and I consider the modes of writing, the array of voices, and the social perspectives that might emerge when we sense that our lives are embedded in the lives of others.

My students and I explore negotiations of the auto/biographical demand in various genres. We interpret, for example, Jamaica Kincaid's (1990) short story "Mariah," June Jordan's (2002) essay "Report from the Bahamas," Adrienne Rich's (1984) poem "Splittings," and Jane Wagner and Tina DiFeliciantonio's (1997) documentary film *Girls Like Us.* With these texts, my students and I develop language to help us locate the auto/biographical demand in our own writing. Ultimately we seek understanding of the rhetorical forms we use to manage the way others appear in our narratives. Working through my experience of the auto/biographical demand brought me to the subject and title of this book, awakening me to the call of place in self-formation. If "place" for me is an intellectual passion, an endlessly fascinating concept and pathway into speculation, it is also a rhetorical form that organizes my perception of self and other. For this book, I have written about authors, critics, fictional characters, and family members whose passionate attachments to place have helped disclose the meaning of my own. I read my self through the lens of place, drawing on its complexities to expand my autobiographical vision.

Working Through Place As a Cultural Symptom

The concept of working-through at the foundation of this research is specifically psychoanalytic. J. Laplanche and J.-B. Pontalis (1973) define working-through as the "psychical work" by which individuals acknowledge repressed content and free themselves from "the grip of mechanisms of repetition" (p. 488). Working-through requires the interpretation of symptoms or unconsciously repeated patterns along with the subject's recognition of an interpretation in various contexts. This work encourages the individual "to pass from rejection or merely intellectual acceptance" of repressed or denied elements to an understanding of these elements within lived experience (p. 488).

Freud developed the notion of working-through along with the other fundamental concepts of psychoanalysis in terms of individual psychology, but the value of these concepts for understanding social formations and processes should not be underestimated. Dominick LaCapra (1997) describes the social character of Freudian concepts, reminding us that they "refer to processes that always involve modes of interaction, mutual reinforcement, conflict, censorship, [and] orientation toward others" (p. 80). Working-through, a more general term for the process of mourning, LaCapra continues, "may obviously take collective forms, for example, in rituals" (p. 80). LaCapra enriches this example with a discussion of Pierre Nora's sites of memory. "*Lieux de mémoire*," he writes, "may be *lieux de trauma* as well as commemorative sites, and the question is whether and how they may become *lieux de deuil* [mourning] for working through traumatic events" (p. 80).

LaCapra (1997) thus posits the psychical processing of historical experience, a manner of working-through that fosters social change. Necessary for the movement from collective trauma to collective mourning (or working-through) is an acknowledgment of the specificity of the losses involved. To contribute to practices of social justice, a collective process of working-through must acknowledge the specificity of the varying and historically translated traumas of victims and perpetrators. Indeed, an important element of "public debate and education should be," LaCapra (1997) argues, "the attempt to define what is indeed a genuine loss worthy of mourning and what should be not mourned but vigorously criticized and emotionally given the response it deserves" (p. 103). Significantly, as LaCapra theorizes it, this process must come to form between public and private spheres, requiring collective efforts to confront and understand the past as well as individual efforts to find the patterns of history in one's subjective experience.[2] In psychoanalytic terms, such a process would offer "a homeopathic socialization or ritualization of the repetition-compulsion," one that potentially "counteract[s] compulsiveness by re-petitioning in ways that allow for critical distance, change, resumption of social life, and renewal" (p. 81).

With this research, I hope to contribute to such a process of working-through Southern history. Toward that goal, I explore a cultural symptom—an overdetermined attachment to place—that blocks social-psychoanalytic movement in the region. Because that attachment is unconscious, the redolent pleasures of fusion (what Freud called the "oceanic feeling") re-enforce an infantile need to merge with the co-current place, and to suspend it in a moment of unperturbed harmony. To break with the "place" as origin would instigate a set of reactions tantamount to traumatic loss. Defending against this loss, my analysis shows, requires a victim; it also blocks the movement of desire necessary for the resymbolization of experience (Silverman, 2000). In other words, as the white South clings to a fantasy of place, it continues its subjugation of black men and women and forestalls the psychoanalytic and educative process that might unmoor us from this history of social violence. To disclose what underlies the cultural symptom of Southern place, I explore it historically and autobiographically, demonstrating the psychical work of recognizing a particular subjective pattern in multiple social contexts. In this process, I bring focus to the experiences of white men. I do so not to reinstate the power of white men who are beleaguered by loss but to expose and critique responses to this loss, responses that obscure injustices in Southern history worthy of mourning.

The White Male Subject in Southern Literature

In the novel *Go Down, Moses,* William Faulkner (1942/1990) provides a key example of the white male Southerner's problematic attachment to place. The novel's main character, Ike McCaslin, has an abiding faith in the "wilderness, the big woods, bigger and older than any recorded document," a realm feared by men but serving as a "refuge and sanctuary of liberty and freedom" (pp. 183, 271). Though deeply attached to the wilderness, Ike is ultimately ambivalent about the Southern land. As the land becomes tamed, owned, and cultivated, as its "edges [are] constantly and punily gnawed at by men with plows and axes" (p. 185), Ike sees the evils of society prevailing over the purity of the wilderness. Attached to an idealized wilderness, Ike ultimately repudiates the "tamed land" he inherits because it represents the "sins of the father," the racism and sexual violence of white men in Southern history.

By repudiating the land, Ike maintains his ideal of the wilderness, a symbol of purity that palliates guilt. As Schreiber (2001) argues, "Ike struggles to free himself from his cultural and familial inheritance by relinquishing individual responsibility and escaping to a 'purer' world of solitude, based on his idea of the woods" (p. 23). Clarifying the link between the purity of Southern place and the white male subject, Schreiber continues: "[Ike] inherits the wilderness as his object of desire from his roots in the South, and it sustains his identity as a Southern white male" (p. 23). The narratives that I interpret in the following chapters address Ike McCaslin's predicament, implicitly and explicitly. They address a crisis of white masculinity born of a belief in the purity of identity and place. The work of the Nashville Agrarians exemplifies the most vehement white male attachment to the land, and the contemporary literature I investigate disrupts the alignment of Southern place with the white male subject. My own autobiographical narratives demonstrate a process of working through the cultural attachment to place.

Chapters and Autobiographical Interludes

This book begins with one of several "Autobiographical Interludes" in which I explore various dimensions of my experience of place. In these sections, I depict the power of place to immerse us in memory and provide our lives with a sense of personal meaning, and I reflect on the way "a language of the landscape" contains and potentially obscures the past. My narratives reveal a struggle to negotiate the boundary between home and the social world, the embedding of the social world in subjective experience, and the tension between my self-formation and Southern place. They represent personal entanglements, sometimes with little critical distance. If at times they seem bound up with the Imaginary, with a longing for coherence and self-presence, they adumbrate issues that I work through with more critical distance in the main chapters. These narratives demonstrate what I understand to be the necessary autobiographical dimension of a social-psychoanalytic curriculum.

In Chapter 1, "The American South: Subjective and Social Terrain," I explore social and psychological conditions crucial to understanding a curriculum of place in the American South. This chapter represents the persistence of racism in the region and the difficulty of addressing the issue of racism in educational contexts. I then turn to psychoanalytic theory to provide a framework for understanding the relationship between subjectivity and the social world. Following the work of Judith Butler (1997, 2003), Stephen Frosh (2002a, 2002b), and Kaja Silverman (2000), I provide analysis of subjectivity, social conflict, and the experience of otherness that grounds my understanding of the way autobiographies of place might foster social change. I conclude Chapter 1 with an account of the historical link between Southern place and white patriarchal culture. This history clarifies why the subject of place is indispensable to the social-psychoanalytic study of the region.

In Chapter 2, "Southern Place: Autochthony, White Masculinity, and Southern Aberrations," I review the concept of place in Southern studies. This review focuses on the concept of the "autochthonous ideal," a concept Donald Davidson used to articulate the relationship between the Southern writer and Southern place. I show how the autochthonous ideal supports a monolithic vision of the American South and diminishes our capacity to understand social diversity, confront subjective conflict, and work toward social change. I then provide an account of a perceived "crisis of place" in the South and explore the social-psychoanalytic value of emphasizing our difficulties with life in the region. Reading such difficulties in the work of Davidson, a central figure in the Nashville Agrarians movement, allows me to address more specifically the way the traditional conception of Southern place supports white masculinity. Davidson's relationship to Marshallville, Georgia, in particular, allows me to examine the cultural power of the Agrarians' romantic rural aesthetic and to expose an "anxiety of insufficiency" (DiPiero, 2002, p. 9) at work in the Southern white man's attachment to place.

In Chapter 3, "The Strange Limbo of Southern Place," I interpret the work of two contemporary writers, Randall Kenan (1992) and Reginald McKnight (1998), who disrupt the traditional conception of Southern place. Kenan's "Run, Mourner, Run" and McKnight's "The White Boys" take up and transform the Agrarian image of the white male subject in his relationship to land and landscape. In different ways, these writers depict the psychological entanglements of Southern white men. They also unmoor us from the South's binding "sense of place" and compel our reconceptualization of the "ground" on which Southern place rests. Kenan and McKnight thus provide a means for rethinking the construction of white male identity and for attending to the voices, identifications, and desires that the hegemonic form of that identity has repressed.

In Chapter 4, "Reshaping our Inherited Landscape," I interpret the work of two contemporary Southern writers, Yusef Komunyakaa and Ellen Douglas, who refigure the traditional conception of Southern place by using a language of the landscape to address the traumas of the past. These writers emphasize a process of working through painful experiences and unconscious meanings for the purpose of social change. In doing so, they disrupt the image of the autochthonous Southern writer, marking Southern place as significant ground for social-psychoanalytic inquiry. In the poetry and essays of Yusef Komunyakaa (1993, 2002a, 2002b, 2003), an African American writer, we see the emotional complexity necessary for rethinking Southern place. Komunyakaa's negotiation of place emerges as a powerful confrontation with the color line. In Ellen Douglas's (1979/1994) novel *The Rock Cried Out,* we see white male subjectivity compelled to negotiate questions of racial difference and racist history. Douglas directly responds to the Agrarian tradition. She thus enables us to imagine the construction of Southern places that do not remain enthralled to the region's historical trauma or bound by the narcissistic projections of those in positions of cultural dominance. Chapter 4 illuminates a form of autobiographical curriculum inquiry that can help us expand our vision of self and society and contribute to the progressive reconstruction of the American South.

AUTOBIOGRAPHICAL INTERLUDE

A Nascent Language about Our Shared World

As abiding and expansive presence, place outlasts much that vanishes.

—Edward Casey (1993, p. 310)

As place endures, it remembers. Place holds the past when we lose our sense of connection to what has gone before. When something shocks the binding of our everyday world, obscuring the relation between the self we have been and the one we are becoming, our surroundings have the potential to return the vital memories nested in them.

However, as psychoanalysis teaches, the return of what is lost or forgotten is as likely to dislocate as it is to renew a sense of self. The past haunts the places we inhabit. And the ghosts we confront in them are, as Christopher Bollas (2000) reminds us, projected and potentially disturbing aspects of ourselves. Our surroundings thus evoke that which nourishes as well as that which shatters our sense of being-in-the-world.

I discover this paradoxical character of place when I visit my grandfather's farm and contemplate the family history it holds. In the 1950s my grandfather began raising horses on a secluded plot of land in Baton Rouge, Louisiana. Farming was not his livelihood. He nonetheless spent much of his life in the solitude of this farm's rural landscape. The land my grandfather cultivated was not only a personal retreat but also a gift to his children and grandchildren, who struggled to communicate with each other outside the concerns of a family business. His commitment to the farm and the symbolic nature of his gift—a gift of place and an appeal for connectedness—invite my reflection on the way place informs and even replaces the fragile language that connects us to self and others.

After my grandfather's death a few years ago, I began to learn how he suffered a sense of distance from many in the family. What I saw as his austereness now appears to be the weight of frustrated communication. What I saw as his dedication to the farm now seems to represent the displacement of emotions from difficult relationships. I feel a deep affinity with him, as I recognize how my research into place discloses my own desire to secure ground in the face of confusion and loss.

Many in the family visit the farm to recover lost connections. Over the years, it has become a symbol of familial harmony and coherence to me, signifying a measure of congeniality between my father and his siblings, who live their workdays together in the tensions of their family business. Since my youth, we gathered at the farm for family events—for birthdays, picnics, and my grandparents' anniversary. We now speak of our days there with fondness and nostalgia, remembering the farm as the background of our unfolding lives. Like my grandfather, we fished in the lake bordered by a great thickness of woods, lingered in the yellowing grass of the farm's vast and craggy field, and watched a herd of Shetland ponies fill the landscape with unpredictable movement. Sharing this place helped us negotiate familial connections other places could never seem to nurture. To me it now embodies my grandfather's wish for deeper communication with those closest to him as well as my family's struggle to create clearer meaning from inexpressible conflicts. More important, it evokes my own struggle to connect and create. In the solitude of the farm's landscape, whose forms and contours I know deeply fascinated and inspired my grandfather, I am able to reconsider much that lies in the folds of my family's past. To me, the farm is a place where we have struggled individually with a nascent language about our shared worlds. It has therefore come to signify the work of articulating the most elusive parts of the self and being with others.

My grandfather's relationship to his farm and my redoubling it in memory indicate something significant about the role of place in self-formation. The power of place to bind and sway subjectivity resides in the subtlety and complexity of its influence. If, as Casey (1993) suggests, place is a substantial force on subjectivity, one that stands in, to some degree, for our inevitable experiences of loss and change, the force remains largely unconscious. We consciously apprehend only fragments of our experiences of place. And these fragments are an amalgamation of memories, narratives, emotions, and images. Our experience of place can thus create as many uncertainties as it assuages, and pose as many questions—personal and communal—as it answers. This subtlety and complexity draw me to the subject of place as the foundation for curriculum theorizing.

As my reflection on my grandfather's farm indicates, places we know intimately can immerse us in memory. They have the potential to exalt thinking and the imagination. And they can provide a sense of continuity to our life history.

But the personal meanings we derive from and attribute to place can also limit reflection on our lives in the world. The sense that a place ineluctably "contains" a plenitude of personal meaning is more likely to forestall rather than promote awareness of our call into a culturally and politically complex world. As "an abiding and expansive presence" that "outlasts much that vanishes," place—that is, our experience of "being-in-place" (Casey, 1993)—can indeed help us make meaning of our lives. However, in contemporary society, our senses of place have been called on more and more to compensate for the pain of living in a seemingly placeless world (Casey, 2001a). When our relationships to place palliate rather than help us work through conditions of displacement and self-estrangement, they damage rather than enrich our relationship to the public sphere.

A significant part of my growing up privileged in South Louisiana is that I was afforded a great deal of space and solitude for contemplating my experience. Given to such contemplation, I learned to trust the capacity of various places to satiate my desire for personal meaning in the face of life's disturbing opacities. My grandfather's farm, my spacious room, the woods behind my home, the Cane River basin of North Louisiana, and the many sites of my family's sojourning on the Gulf Coast all contributed to my sense of a perpetual ground of being, a perpetual "here" holding my life together.

In her novel *The Rock Cried Out,* the Southern writer Ellen Douglas (1979/1994) captures just such a relationship to place, one in which the landscape is internalized as the guardian of personal identity. Remarking on his relationship to the natural surroundings of his homeplace, the novel's main character, Alan McLaurin, explains: "Any place, any time you can tell yourself romantic stories and try to live in them" (p. 79). Alan exemplifies this practice of inhabiting idealized self-narratives as he speaks of traveling in the woods and coming across a spring and cistern he has never seen before. While gazing upon the water "clear and icy, welling up under the noon sun and rolling the glittering bronze sand," Alan discovers a "battered dipper still hung by a rusty chain from a ring in one of the locust posts" (p. 80). The evidence that other human beings inhabit the woods invites Alan's identification rather than his expectation of difference and gives him cause to imagine a benevolence and domesticity in the wilderness. He continues,

> I drank and walked homeward in deep silence through the woods, imagining myself a traveler who found that spring in a country he had never walked through before, who drank and walked on, alert for smoke from the chimney of a wilderness home and the sight of the man who had chained the dipper there. (p. 80)

Alan's perspective on place compels him to translate the new and strange into the familiar and protective. It reduces the complex tension between place and subjectivity to a secure bond between self and world. Examining place autobiographically, I have come to recognize how an unconscious desire for a seamless self/world relationship diminishes my own capacity for relating to others and myself.

CHAPTER 1

The American South: Subjective and Social Terrain

Introduction

Although places enable us to rethink our personal histories, they also hold collective histories that exceed and imbue our subjective experiences of place. In the American South, where there is "an intensified relation to place" (Pinar, 2004, p. 95), place experiences bear, explicitly and implicitly, the region's history of racism and biracial culture. Inquiries into place, therefore, can serve the renegotiation of race relations and can ground the process of social reconstruction in the South (Pinar, 2004). Although Southern writers such as Ellen Douglas, William Faulkner, Trudier Harris, Eudora Welty, and Richard Wright have revealed the way race relations are embedded in the experience of place, a Southern "sense of place" has historically served white Southerners in their denial of the racism and inhumanity at the foundations of the region's history and culture. What results is an overdetermined sense of place in Southern literature, criticism, and everyday discourse—an impediment to rather than a source of social understanding.[3]

Scott Romine (1999) outlines the psychosocial process by which the South came to signify a "concrete" community and an "objective social world" (p. 9). He cites James McBride Dabbs, who asserts that through "a process of violent abstraction, we [white Southerners] converted the African Negro into the image of our desire, a slave" (quoted in Romine, 1999, p. 9). Dabbs thus captures a translation of desire from eros into the subaltern's poverty and suffering. Romine elaborates, explaining that because "it is unbearable to live with an abstraction" (an abstraction of one's own desire, I would emphasize), the white South assuaged its self-alienation through a fantasy of Southern place as a "concrete object."

The white South thus "deferred reflection" on the origins of white Southern community "for fear of what it might reveal," that is, its own guilt and inhumanity (p. 9). A mangled desire, a denial of racial violence, and the sublimation of this desire and violence as a belief in the solidity of community—these are the underlying features of what Dabbs calls the "massive, concrete South" (quoted in Romine, 1999, p. 9). Thus, if a conception of place is to serve the South in its social reconstruction, this fact cannot be ignored and will have to be incorporated into any plan for restitution. The region's history of racist violence pervades the natural and human landscape, and it can lure us into destructive forms of culture and community.

Hence, an overdetermined conception of place removes actual Southern places from "the living tissue of their moment in time" (Gray, 2000, p. 501), supporting the fantasy of a singular and monolithic prior South, one that can elide mutability. Faulkner, perhaps more than any author, represents the desire to memorialize achieved moments of a past time, a time when some kind of centralized collective fantasy of supremacy was actively gratified; he captured the white South's effort to avoid confrontation with the present—a present that is not only transitory but also decentralized. To unsettle the fantasy of a continuous, harmonious past embodied in Southern sites, we will have to deconstruct place "as a stable site of tradition and history" (Ladd, 2002, p. 56). In fact, we will have to embrace a construction of place that is, as Barbara Ladd explains, "provisional, more fleeting, more subversive, and likewise more creative—a locus for economic, political, discursive, and more broadly cultural transactions, a site of memory and meaning both for the past and the future" (p. 56).

To grasp the significance of Southern place in our experience, therefore, we cannot remain within the subsoil of the self; in fact, we must plumb deeper. Place memory is personal *and* collective, subjective *and* social. To explore this fact, Lippard (1997) encourages us to think of "each view [of place], no matter how banal, [as] a palimpsest." In doing so, she suggests, we might begin to understand the sociopolitical character of the places that "penetrate our lives and memories most intensely"; that is, we might see how they are "composed of mythologies, histories, and ideologies—the stuff of identity and representation" (p. 33).

In this chapter, I explore the process and problems of grasping place as subjective and social terrain. I then depict the social and psychological conditions we must consider as we attempt to renew educational contact with the personal and collective histories Southern place bears.

Negotiating Knowledge of the Racist Past and Present

From the middle passage, through slavery and the civil rights movement, to our present and embedded "culture of segregation" (Hale, 1998), racist practices have been translated from more overt forms into intricate patterns in the social field. Our racist past is with us and is nearer to the surface of our everyday lives than the historical translation might suggest. Racism persists even alongside the greatest support for cultural diversity because unconscious desire and fantasy complicate the way we comprehend racial identity and race relations (Lane, 1998). Where racism remains opaque in seemingly innocuous personal and educational practices, we postpone the crucial work of integrating into our self-concepts knowledge of our most destructive and anti-democratic impulses.

Time and again white Southerners have covered over these contradictions in their identities, rendering internal strife as racial prejudice, stereotype, and violence (Hale, 1998; Pinar, 2001; Williamson, 1984). In this psychosocial landscape, where conditions of oppression go ignored, white Southerners have furthered their own alienation from self and history. The estrangement has no doubt diminished their lives. Its most destructive force, however, has been delivered into the lives of African American women and men. It is crucial, therefore, that we disclose the white psychological investment in a class system that maintains a "black underclass." White fantasy attaches to black experience in devastating ways. Though many argue to the contrary, abandoning to the margins of consciousness knowledge of the racist past and present does not enable more efficient routes to democratic dialogue and intellectual development. Learning must address the glaring inequities of a social system so that educational renewal can occur. The refusal to address the way racism structures the social field and our individual lives is the very antithesis of learning.

As a teacher in the South, I am concerned with the way this refusal functions within my own experience and the conversations I have with my students. I have spoken of the South as my home but recognize that I live in and pass through many Souths, including places where knowledge of racism is violently refused and places where Southerners, white and black, attempt to renegotiate the terms of our shared history. This variation is also true of the classrooms in which I have learned and taught. Through my research and teaching, I attempt to disrupt the discourses that advance racist perspectives and to foster spaces amenable to anti-racist dialogue. This work intensifies my experience of my own race and gender identity.

As a Southern white man, I have come to understand that my sense of self is in some part founded on my need to avoid social disparity; so long as it remains hidden from consciousness, I need not address it in my life or my teaching. In my youth, for example, when I witnessed racist events, I experienced them as temporary magnifications of difference, as events that did not implicate me personally. Imagining myself untouched by this intense marking of the social field, I became interested in race and racism at a distance—as experiences of others rather than as something having an effect on my own identity. However, now, in my memory of such experiences, I can see my own entanglement with white cultural fantasy, with the white fantasy of the otherness of race and the white liberal fantasy of the otherness of racism. However, by acknowledging these entanglements and working through them autobiographically, I can confront both an impasse in self-understanding and a broader cultural struggle, the struggle to bring questions of racial justice to the public sphere in the South (see Pinar, 2004).

To maintain the status quo, Southern educators often refuse to confront systemic racism. All too often it serves as the ground of pedagogy and classroom communication. The preservice teachers with whom I work, students significantly resistant to discussions of race, indicate in their autobiographical writing how their educational experiences support such resistance. Alongside discussions of specific instances of racism in their families and communities, they describe schooling in which the subject of racism, if mentioned at all, appears as an archaic problem. For many of them, to engage the question of racism is to risk failed language, emotional excess, and loss of identity. One student explains that she and other white students face a "frustration with differences" that inevitably causes "difficulty in communication" (Beth, 2001). Another explains that "feeling shameful" makes "race a very sensitive subject for me to write and talk about in academic settings" (Lindsay, 2001). Another student struggling to understand how to work through her prejudices contemplates the relation between political and psychological liberation. She cites a passage in which Maxine Greene associates "freedom" with "acceptance." The student then writes: "This association strikes me as true, but I still wonder: acceptance of what?" Suggesting the binding power of the refusal I have described, this student answers: "acceptance that freedom is an ongoing process, whether one seeks freedom from oppression or my own prison of self" (Julie, 2001).

My students' autobiographies of place reveal the South's embedded pedagogy of racial difference. In many ways, their educational experiences correspond to my own. My knowledge of racial difference was inscribed in my earliest parental identifications, and outside my family that knowledge usually met a dense social fabric of racist discourse. The schools I attended most often taught that racism was something suffered in the past. And the schools where I have worked since 1994 are in a community that just recently settled a forty-year-old desegregation injunction— "settled" only after mass "white flight" from the schools. In this context, I want to help cultivate a public conversation about racial justice. This requires knowledge of the way we have obscured the subject of racial oppression and accepted it as an immutable fact of the social world. I understand the pursuit of such knowledge to be painful work. With this, I am compelled to approach learning as a means of understanding *why* those who enjoy power refuse to confront social realities. In this intransigence, we do see the effort to secure the rewards of superiority. But what reasons might we find running deeper? Psychological investments in the power of a collective vision, or master narrative, keep that vision or narrative ongoing, even as it remains detrimental and destructive to society as a whole. Through a deconstructive lens, we may ask not only how systems of knowledge structure our lives, but also how a refusal of knowledge structures our lives? And how might the study of Southern place dislodge this refusal, helping us to acknowledge the racist past and present and move toward healthier dialogue about social justice?

Social and Subjective Terrain

In *After Words: The Personal in Gender, Culture, and Psychotherapy,* Stephen Frosh (2002a) elaborates on the relationship between subjectivity and the social world:

> Subjecthood arises out of the constructs made available in the culture, pulled together through the immersion of each one of us in a complex of relationships and ideologically inscribed positions. As this happens, as subjects are produced, so we become language users, power wielders, active and agentic, but nevertheless reflections of the social processes out of which we have been formed. (p. 156)

As suggested earlier, the concept of place, when theorized in its complexity, discloses the psychosocial tension Frosh describes. My students and I examine place autobiographically to illuminate the interrelationship between social context and subjective experience. We explore our experiences as we inhabit and move between home, school, nature, art, and community. We identify the conventional boundaries to these places and attempt to articulate the conventionally unmarked connections between them. Our autobiographies of place thus unsettle the sense that personal experience is a hermetic private realm and the social world an immutable backdrop to our lived worlds.

Through our autobiographies of place, my students and I seek understanding of Judith Butler's (2003) argument that "at the most intimate levels, we are social" (p. 32). To grasp ourselves as subjects of complex places, we attempt to confront the way social codes and imperatives infuse self experience.[4] Butler reminds us that "when we are speaking about the 'subject' we are not always speaking about an individual: we are [often] speaking about a model for agency and intelligibility" (p. 32). Following Butler, I ask students to question how our individual subjectivities relate to cultural "models" that are "based on notions of sovereign power" (p. 32). We discuss specifically the models of race and gender subjectivity embedded in Southern culture and how these models impinge on our identities, desires, and educational journeys. Emphasizing both the personal and social dimensions of place, we try to grasp how, as Butler writes, "we are outside ourselves, constituted in cultural norms that precede and exceed us, given over to a set of cultural norms and a field of power that condition us fundamentally" (p. 32).

This analysis of the social formation of subjectivity is necessary to move our autobiographies of place toward issues of social justice. The emphatic nature of Butler's language, however, points us to other concerns. It compels us to ask about subjective movement and change, about the possibility for resisting and undermining the restrictive social codes that bind the worlds we inhabit. It compels us to ask how we find space for the self outside the social dictates embedded in our experience, and whether indeed there is self experience outside the field of power that Butler so cogently describes. The theorists who have responded to these questions most incisively have provided us with some extremely challenging ideas on the relationship between subjectivity and society.[5] This theory further grounds my understanding that we must learn to recognize and articulate the way our lives are interwoven with our social surroundings. Yet it also raises my awareness of the risk suggested by my students' questions. When we think about our individual subjectivities as fundamentally conditioned (to paraphrase Butler), we risk treating the self as a passive imprint of cultural norms, as an object incapable of movement and change. Through this thinking, we confront our ambivalence about subjectivity's immersion in and emergence from the social world.

This problem leads me to a more specifically psychoanalytic reading of the formation of subjectivity. When we perceive the self as a static form, we exclude awareness of the unconscious. Though we have an enduring capacity to create meaning, the meanings that bear on the self endlessly exceed our grasp. Theorists of Lacanian psychoanalysis in the context of learning (Alcorn, 2002; Bracher, 2000; Frosh, 2002a) argue that confronting the fact of this excess is necessary for understanding and compelling subjective movement and change.

The excess these theorists describe is an effect of the Symbolic and the Real, the registers of subjectivity that undermine the ego. I want to elaborate on the theory of these registers as it informs my understanding of autobiographical inquiry. Lacan describes the subject inhabiting a social symbolic field through which it comes into being. The subject can only illusorily master this system of language. Within the Symbolic, the subject occupies discourses that arise around particular terms of value called master signifiers. The subject seeks stability in its identification with master signifiers yet remains subject to and divided by the unconscious, "the significatory excess of language" (Dean, 1991, p. 19). The subject therefore depends on a realm of meaning that ensures meaning and subjective identity will never be complete.

In *World Spectators,* Kaja Silverman (2000) theorizes this incompleteness as a fundamental loss in psychic life, one that inaugurates desire and compels the creation of meaningful psychical (libidinal) connections. Silverman's argument relies on Lacan's theory of the Real. As I stated above, the Real refers to bodily states and affects that exceed both our capacity to make meaning in language and the sense of self-coherence we gain through visual perception of our surroundings. Though the Symbolic (the social symbolic field of meaning) exceeds consciousness, its meanings are potentially if not totally articulable. The Real, on the other hand, is fundamentally inexpressible. It undermines or shatters all language and the self that is moored there. As the mark of the inexpressible, the Real can help us theorize what remains outside society's imprint on subjectivity.

The Real originates from our relationship to the maternal body as an undifferentiated flux of sensations. It thus precedes ego formation and symbolic identification with parental figures and social norms. Once we have acceded to a place in language—a coded position in the social symbolic network—the Real persists within subjectivity as the register of our deepest desires and anxieties (Bracher, 2000, pp. 161–165).

In much Southern fiction, the Real is perceived as a fearful registry of what can't be controlled by signification and difference. In fact, violence and violation in

Faulkner are typically described in terms in which it is clear that a stable language has broken down. What rears up in its place is the inexplicable Real that haunts many of Faulkner's restless characters—Quentin Compson, for example, for whom the problem of time introduces the Real, driving him, despite his father's warning, to spend his "breath trying to conquer it" (Faulkner, 1929, p. 93).

The register of the Real confronts us with the most intractable problems of experience. As the psychical remainder of our merger with the maternal body, the Real functions in experience as an unnamable loss. We suffer the Real as a radical void. As the fundamental loss within subjectivity, the Real also founds our capacity to cathect new love objects. It is the "non-object" or "lack" we allow objects and others in the world to embody (Silverman, 2000). This will be particularly relevant to understanding the connection between subjectivity and place. We experience the Real not only as lack but also as an affirmation of our capacity to connect, as the foundation of desire. Finally, though the Real enables desires consistent with the ego, it also stirs our desire in ways that society and our conscious identifications disallow. As Mark Bracher (1993) explains, aspects of our "Real jouissance [enjoyment] . . . *are in themselves antithetical* to the positions we have set up in our ego ideal" (p. 48, emphasis in original). We therefore experience the Real paradoxically—as a source of trauma, the cause of desire, and a threat of dissolution.

Originating from our relationship to the maternal body, the Real functions within our self/other relationships. It is the inexpressible remainder of our immersion in a social world. Frosh (2002a) emphasizes the social origins and effects of the Real:

> So the ambivalence in the culture, the poisoned chalice it holds, is part of its power and is inserted into the subjects which it creates, not necessarily as a clear statement, but as a "leftover" or sense of trouble. Being constitutive, it is obscure to the subject out of which it is made; as with any system of which one is a member, it is difficult to find a place to stand in order to speak of it directly. (p. 156)

Following Frosh, I encourage reflection on the elusive elements of our experiences of place. This reflection complicates the perception that being-in-place secures self-presence, and it unsettles, or questions, the idea that our place in the world precedes being-in-the-world with others (Casey, 1996; Hooper, 2001; Richardson, 2002). This model is essentially a postmodern one in which the self is always precipitated by an image of a social other and how that other constructs it. The same can be said about place: place constructs us as much as we construct it; an image of place, although unreal or fictional, can be the template on which other narratives of place, and the self, are written. When my students and I think of our shared world in terms of place, we posit it to be a site of past events and experiences as well as a contemporary nexus of social codes and practices (Mitchell, 2002a). Moreover we question the apparent stability of our own place within school and society and ask what the experience of otherness that place produces might mean for our lives as educators in the American South.

Otherness and the Play of Meaning

Elusiveness is part of the play of meaning.

—Michael Eigen (1992, p. 31)

Michael Eigen calls us to consider how a tolerance for the unknown is necessary for creative thought. His comment on the elusiveness of meaning appears in a discussion of structure and change in psychic life—what he calls the "plasticity and persistence of the self" (p. 30). As a psychoanalyst writing from the heart of therapeutic experience, Eigen is concerned with a self that is both shaped and shattered by a sense of otherness, a self animated and disturbed by that which eludes it. With the phrase "the play of meaning" Eigen refers specifically to a psychoanalytic conception of language. "As Lacan emphasized," Eigen writes, "language itself provides structure and slipperiness as signifiers slide like colors into each other" (p. 31). The instability of language makes communication a process not only of creating significance but also of negotiating that which is other to significance. As Eigen remarks on the generative force of the disjunction between the psyche and linguistic meaning, he urges us toward a writing practice of discovery, challenging us to consider how we might inhabit language with respect for the experiences of incertitude and inexpressibility.

I have felt these experiences acutely in my investigations of the American South. The South is beyond my grasp if I do not address the region's racism and sexism. Yet inquiring into the way these ideologies bind the South and my experience of home, I tap into the complex ways I am implicated in them, a mode of discovery that does not readily translate into insight. The "dynamics of implication," Alice Pitt (2003) explains, "blur boundaries between self and other, between conscious and unconscious messages, and between objective reality and theoretical construction" (p. 7). By discovering my implication in the injustices and forms of social hatred particular to the South, I lose a sense of the boundary between those social realities I abhor and my own life narrative. I witness my self in a broader frame but also glimpse the way my self persists through a process of exclusion.

Identities are created in part by what they exclude (Butler, 1997; Fuss, 1995). Through my autobiographical research, I have become concerned with the political force of excluded race and gender knowledge. I want to address the educational problem of negotiating gaps in knowledge that represent opacities in the self. How does one create insight from knowledge that undermines one's sense of identity? How does one create insight from knowledge that undermines one's sense of having a capacity to know? My own discovery of self-implication challenges my sense of being at home in the South. The elusiveness from which I now seek to create meaning, therefore, is both a force of language and an element of place. What can these two experiences of dislocation—from language and from place—learn from each other?

In *World Spectators,* Silverman (2000) offers an image of the individual inhabited *by the world* to distinguish the *being-in-the-world* that owns the social, historical, and ecological foundations of the self. She writes: "We are not in the world merely by virtue of being born into it: indeed, most of us are not really in the world at all. Paradoxical as it may sound, we are only really in the world when it is in us—when we have made room within our psyches for it to dwell and expand" (p. 29). According to Wallace Stevens (1965), it takes imagination to grasp reality, and "the imagination loses vitality as it ceases to adhere to what is real" (p. 6). Similarly, Silverman traces the dynamism of subjectivity to an inter-inhabitation of self and situation. One's place in the world—one's situatedness among and influence on other "creatures and things" (p. 30)—she suggests, becomes a question of the way otherness is allowed to reside in the psyche. With this, Silverman frames the psychosocial process of promoting rather than repudiating the indwelling of otherness.

Through its spatial metaphor, this formulation of being-in-the-world points to the problem of uncovering the influential and binding elements of place. Where Silverman implies a failure to make psychical space for the world or worlds in which we live, I think of the South that is my home, a place whose history and social reality continue to be obscured and distorted by white male fantasy. I think of the way many inhabit the South, connecting (often fervently) identity to place but at the cost of and in resistance to knowledge of the various forms of bigotry that pervade the region. I think of my own struggle to understand how that bigotry shapes my own experience. If politically responsible being-in-the-world requires a psychical indwelling of the world in its complexity, then what are we to do with those forms of inhabiting the world—racism, sexism, homophobia—that are bent on repelling any disturbance of otherness? Moreover, what is the nature of the otherness for which we are challenged to make psychical space?

Silverman (2000) suggests that what is radically other yet available to consciousness is our "language of desire" (p. 39). More specifically, following Lacan, she argues that through our object choices, we unconsciously accumulate a "complex and multifaceted constellation of signifiers" that represent our entire history of desire and the foundation for our future desires (p. 39). Silverman elaborates this dynamic by explaining that each subject enters the symbolic—the realm of social signification—through a loss that also initiates desire. The loss, she continues, is actually twofold: the loss of self-presence or being and the loss of the first love object—the latter inaugurating the desire to fill the irreducible void of the former. One negotiates this "lack of being" through language and further libidinal object choices. To summarize, Silverman explains that the loss of being—of unity or totality—cannot be symbolized and thus founds "the human imperative to engage in a ceaseless signification" (p. 146). By "ceaseless signification," she means not only speaking and writing—that is, conscious uses of language; she refers also to our unconscious libidinal language. "Each new libidinal object," Silverman writes, "provides [the lack of being] with lineaments and a face, transforms the 'nothing' into a 'something'" (p. 39). Paraphrasing Freud, Silverman emphasizes that each love object is "a radically heterogeneous collocation of memories, to all of which we could never have simultaneous access" (p. 41). Thus, we carry within our conscious search for meaning the residue of our libidinal histories, a language that is other to consciousness.

Frosh (2002b) also provides insight into the question of otherness. In particular, he elaborates on the psychoanalytic concept of "the other" and its relation to racial and ethnic hatred. "What exactly," Frosh asks, "might be the characteristics of, or at least ascribed to, otherness in general, and why does it so strain the tolerance of the self?" (p. 392). Drawing on several theorists, Frosh argues that otherness is a difference that is both external to and at the "unconscious core" of subjectivity. He further argues that otherness is "a continuing causal force . . . in psychic life," a force with the capacity to comfort, inspire, and agitate the self (pp. 405–406). Concerned with the foundations of racial and ethnic hatred, Frosh brings the agitated and "distressed" self/other relation to the fore. His conceptual analysis, therefore, helps us to see otherness not merely as the subjective experience of other people but more significantly as an enigmatic and potentially disturbing resonance between inner experience and the external world.

Pointing to the malignance of current and historical forms of social hatred, Frosh (2002b) suggests: "[T]he other must mean . . . something from which each one of us cannot escape" (p. 393). Reviewing several attempts at using psychoanalysis to explore the dynamics of racism, Frosh finds that many of these theories, though critically valuable, too often "suggest a relatively clear differentiation between self and other, between what the subject experiences and what the other represents" (p. 392). Michael Rustin, for example, discusses the other as "an empty category" and "the repository of the racist's dark impulses," whereas Joel Kovel treats the other as "a historically constructed symbolic category made to carry the burden of that which is repudiated from the white psyche" (p. 392).[6] Frosh, on the other hand, moves the discussion of "the other" at work in the racist psyche into a conceptual frame that understands otherness to be constitutive of the self and subjectivity. He therefore invites us to consider an ongoing and ineradicable relation to an internal otherness, and therefore to question how and why that relation has become mangled in cases of racial hatred.

Opening the Region's History of Race to the Question of Gender

In the American South, conscious and unconscious structures of racism undermine educational efforts in ways we have yet to fully comprehend. Education must provide a view of social justice; it fails, however, in its lapses of recognition and responsibility. This history of racial abuse is inscribed in the South's collective memory and contemporary social field. Without proper redress of these injustices—that is, without working through its history of slavery, lynching, and institutional racism—the region continues to be subject to politics rooted in white fantasy rather than dedicated to the difficult work of remembering the South's complex racial history. What in particular makes this work difficult, threatening, and intrusive to the white psyche? Why do white people bond with black people in fantasy (Marriott, 1998, p. 429) rather than join with them to lay bare the history of their relationship? How does the white refusal to think about race and racism cling to identifications other than racial ones?

The failure to remember and work through the South's history of racial violence, it is clear to me, finds its most critical support in a rigid gender matrix—through anxious attachments to norms of masculinity, femininity, and heterosexuality. In the South, racism, misogyny, and homophobia come together in a convoluted—but not impenetrable—knot (see Pinar, 2001). Insofar as each of these forms of social hatred involves both overdetermined and vehemently refused identifications, they share the function of carrying interlaced prohibition and desire; these forms of social hatred are, therefore, vehicles of displaced or disavowed wanting and dread (Butler, 1997, p. 136). How are we to conceive of learning and community when so many relationships are plagued with a fear of who one is or whom one might love?

Many working on the subject of cultural memory argue for the political, ethical, and educational importance of remembering violence and subjugation suffered in the past (Simon, Rosenberg, and Eppert, 2000; Morris, 2001). These theorists articulate ways in which memory might address historical trauma, conceptualize the existential and psychological challenges that accompany "difficult knowledge" (Britzman, 1998) of the past, and elaborate patterns of memory and remembrance in terms of curriculum and pedagogy.

Following these writers, I understand that a curriculum of Southern place should, in fact, disclose the way the past inhabits the present, throwing its shadow over the acts we would deem egregious and wrong. I am specifically concerned with racial subjugation in the history of the region and the translation of that history into contemporary practices, modes of thought, and identifications. As I have suggested, although the study of place can help us work through the past, it has obscured historical trauma. To understand this historical translation requires, I believe, close consideration of the gendered character of place. Therefore, reading relationships between gender identifications and racial/racist identifications, I hope to illuminate the South's gendered pedagogy of whiteness and its racialized pedagogy of gender. My primary concern is to show how the demands of the conventional white male psyche limit educational possibilities in the region and how these limits can be broken. I want to suggest that a consciousness of the cloak of the past, when examined autobiographically (both personally and collectively), can help break these limits imposed on education. One of the practical ways we can bring the dark side of the South, heavy with responsibility, into focus for students is to examine literature that reveals the presence of racist history in our lives, work I take up in Chapters 2, 3, and 4. We must allow for the fact that using literature in this way will dislodge students and ourselves ideologically and that we will have to mourn narcissistic idealizations to mobilize social reform and equity. Yet, as this work unsettles embedded modes of identification and self-understanding, it renews our relationship to the past— a past now rendered opaque, threatening, and meaningless to the present. This book, therefore, is an effort to foster capacities for historical understanding in a region whose politics continue to be dominated by white male fantasies and desires.

I recognize that the region's history of gendered racism deeply affects my self-understanding and teaching life. I also understand that, like my students, I have resisted knowledge of race and gender where that knowledge has threatened my sense of ground, where there has seemed only chaos beyond familiar meanings and identifications. Once we have imagined the chaos of an otherness, however, it is already part of the internal life we have hoped to protect. In the chapters that follow, I inquire into this process by which we wall out what already has purchase within the self.

White Southern Identity and Place

To the white Southerners living in the slave society of the nineteenth century, the anti-slavery movement was an enormous threat. Sheldon Hackney (2004) argues that it "created a consciousness of commonality" among whites and that through the perceived threat to whiteness "was invented a mythological people whose mission was to protect a besieged social order" (pp. 188–189). Secession furthered the white South's solidification of and allegiance to "an undifferentiated cultural identity" (O'Brien, 1979, p. 5). And, as Michael O'Brien argues, "[r]econstruction did even more, for it touched the whole question of racial equality and not merely the more local question of slavery" (p. 5).

In this context, Southern place became an object of intense emotional investment, a talisman and shibboleth of white identity politics.[7] Place takes on a heightened significance in Southern literature because it is freighted with the mangled relationships of white patriarchal culture (Yaeger, 2000). The white South, Jon Smith (2002) argues, has fetishized place because of its inability to work through the region's difficult past. The "sense of place" by which white Southerners differentiate themselves from presumably placeless Northerners, and claim heightened connection with the past, has not provided substantial ground for reflection on histories of violence, oppression, and loss. It has instead, Smith explains, "more often tended to reinforce particularly crippling forms of narcissism" (p. 77). Smith argues convincingly that place, reduced to a narrative fetish, serves as a narcissistic mirror to the white South. Moreover, he likens the white South's psychical investment in place to the Lost Cause religion, as both are figures of redemption for the white (male) Southerner's ongoing crisis of identity (p. 77).

In other words, along with "the South as a term of self-identification," the significance of Southern place was "born out of crisis" (Gray, 2000, p. 372). Psychically, the notion of Southern place embodies and compensates for a crisis felt at the level of both race and gender identity (Pinar, 2001, pp. 237–416). The conceptualization of place is, therefore, indispensable to the social-psychoanalytic study of the region. The meaning of place cannot be taken for granted. If place enables us to question the racialized and gendered sense of crisis embedded in Southern regional identification, it also represents "the virtues of rootedness" that keep such questions at bay (Yaeger, 2000, p. 14). A traditional, romantic conception of place supports the region's reactionary race and gender politics and constrains the pursuit of progressive social change.

AUTOBIOGRAPHICAL INTERLUDE

The Language of the Landscape

Last week, I worked with my father in his garden, the place where he seems most comfortable and connected with the world around him. I chose this work because of late I've felt a disturbing distance between him and me. And this distance, this breach, seems related to a distance I frequently feel in my creative efforts and my life of study. So last Sunday morning, I rose at 7 a.m., eased into the car with my father, and rode to his farm in St. Francisville, Louisiana, wondering what insight into my research might come from a day of tilling soil, planting seeds, and harvesting vegetables—from a day of working the earth with a man with whom I feel I've lost touch. What does it mean to lose touch in a relationship in which meaning once seemed fundamentally grounded? And what creative work can be made from the experience of such an unsettling distance?

As we began the thirty-mile journey from Baton Rouge to St. Francisville, my father said very little. He didn't really begin to speak until we were clearly beyond the northern edge of our hometown. Leaving Baton Rouge, we passed the furniture store my father's father started in 1956 and that my father has worked in for nearly forty years. Approaching the store, the "Town and Country Furniture" sign emerged from among the other signs on Airline Highway, as always, as if from a fog—marking, as I imagine it, the mystery of my origins. Airline Highway is U.S. Highway 61; each time I drive to my father's business, I think of Bob Dylan's "Highway 61," a song that mythologizes this American road, and fathers and sons, in densely symbolic language. For me, this is no doubt a site of myth and enigma. The furniture store represents the limits of communication between my father and me; from it, he and I have inherited a bond in which much is submerged, rendered indecipherable.

When my grandfather died three years ago, at the age of 88, he was still working. Since his teens, my father followed my grandfather in his effort to sustain and improve the furniture business. Vigorously pursuing his interests outside of work—in what always appeared to be an attempt to negate his work world—my father created a substantial boundary within his life, reinforcing the emotional distance that already lay between his father and him. The two men, it seems, traded knowledge of each other's hopes and desires for a partnership in commerce. In my thought, the furniture store embodies the untold story of a father and a son, a story I also imagine to be embedded in my father's taciturn nature. Riding with him last week, I wondered how we might translate this unacknowledged force on our relationship into a conversation. And I continue to wonder about the risks and possibilities in transforming such a silence.

As we drove beyond the furniture store and outside of Baton Rouge, my father began to speak. His speech returned us to familiar language—to the language of the landscape. He remarked on the bend of Highway 61 over Thompson Creek, had me keep a lookout for an impressive stretch of dogwood trees running alongside the woods, pointed out some thorny roses covering an old dilapidated fence, reflected on the productivity of a local truck farm, and wondered about the site of a recently burned field—where lush green grass grew up from scorched and ashen ground.

The language of the landscape is the language my father uses to speak what can't be spoken. I began to understand this the week my grandfather died. During our trips to and from the hospital, my father used the landscape to fix his memories, showing me a pecan tree he had played in when he was a child, pointing out the marshy lake area that once swallowed up my grandfather's tractor, and reminding me that years ago, when my grandfather first arrived in Baton Rouge, the land over which we drove was covered in woods. As he speaks of our surroundings, my father makes brief contact with stories I understand to run much deeper than he can reach with words. My father's language of place, a language he has cultivated through years of farming and landscaping, now resounds with the loss of my grandfather. To me this language itself is a kind of silence—not necessarily a form of secrecy but a reticence, the refuge for a story about a father and son, the refuge for a story that doesn't know where to begin.

I am drawn to the silences in my father's language of place. I am therefore patient as we linger in conversation about the landscape, attentive to the thoughts and memories that surface, curious about what we avoid. When I hear my father speak of live oaks and Cherokee roses, the nest of the barn swallow, and the hue of the sky, I think of our personal histories as histories of loss, and I wonder about the particular sense of loss I have inherited—as my father's son and as a white Southern man.

I am drawn to the silences in my father's language because I would like to take up the thread of a story that I know resides there. Within our experience of the textures of the Southern landscape lies the story of our connection to the history and culture of the American South. Engaging with my father's language of place therefore allows me to imagine the telling of untold stories of fathers and sons, not only those personal stories submerged in my father's and grandfather's shared business obligations or those cut off by our differences in disposition, but more important those stories that are indeed histories of race and gender held at bay by generations of white Southern men.

My father's practice of coming to language through the Southern landscape, of course, has a larger history. A review of that history reveals a connection between the experience of loss in the lives of white Southern men and a denial of the experience and history of others. In what follows, I turn to the history of Southern Agrarianism to develop greater insight into the way this discourse has been used to signify the stability and unity of white masculinity. Understanding the race and gender politics of this rural aesthetic, as I show, can inform a progressive educational return to Southern place. From the discourse of Southern landscape and its immersion in our social structures, we can learn much, and teach more. We must try to use our collective community of writers to inform us of what is not only authorial subjectivity but also the mutual ground for group identity. However, we must also understand how group identity becomes a means for social violence, intensifying difference and antagonism between groups.

In the essay "I'll Take My Land: Contemporary Southern Agrarians," Suzanne Jones (2002) elaborates on literary uses of the Southern landscape, pointing out that "for many earlier southern white writers, the southern rural landscape was the repository of nostalgia for lost ways of life, whether it was the plantation fantasy . . . or the segregated agrarian ideal." (p. 12). For William Faulkner and other modern Southern white writers, Jones explains, the rural landscape became a source of "unsettling guilt about a way of life that flourished on the backs of the black people who tilled the land" (p. 121). Whereas black writers most frequently engaged the Southern rural landscape to confront the racist traumas of Southern history, modern white Southern writers became mired in the shadows of their implication in that history (Morrison, 1992).

Urban growth and gentrification in much of the South have not neutralized the power of the rural landscape to enthrall the minds of Southerners. For contemporary African American writers—Ernest Gaines, Randall Kenan, and Dori Sanders, for example—the rural landscape most often serves as a site of inquiry into the South's legacy of racism; for many white Southern writers, the sensuousness of the landscape, its captivating force, continues to give rise to nostalgia and debilitating guilt, and therefore to obstruct historical awareness and a sense of social responsibility.

This ideologically conservative use of the Southern landscape is rooted in the work of the Nashville Agrarians, a group of twelve Vanderbilt University poets and writers, including Allen Tate, John Crowe Ransom, and Robert Penn Warren, who in their conceptualization of the South launched an attack on modern industrialism and called for a return to traditional American values. In 1930 they published the manifesto *I'll Take My Stand,* a volume of essays Richard Gray (2000) characterizes in terms of "a deep distrust of modern times, the longing for a lost rural and traditional order and a usually unstated racial exclusiveness" (p. 102).

The influence of the Southern Agrarians also dominates the 1953 collection *Southern Renascence: The Literature of the Modern South,* a work said by many to have established the field of Southern literary studies. Edited by Louis Rubin and Robert Jacobs, *Southern Renascence,* Gray (2000) explains, is "deeply committed to [Allen] Tate's 'backward glance'"—that is, a consciousness of the past in the present, insofar as the past refers to the war between the North and the South (p. 102). This "backward glance" thus monumentalized a trauma felt by white Southern men. Caught in a nostalgic and melancholic relationship to the past, *Southern Renascence* "responds to . . . contemporary trauma"—the trauma of World War II and the civil rights movement—"by for the most part suppressing it" (p. 102). Rubin and Jacobs's highly influential volume reiterates the Agrarians' vision of Southern place. It therefore perpetuates a rural aesthetic that privileges the experiences and perspectives of white Southern men.

We can witness the intermingling of white male subjectivity and the Southern landscape around conditions of trauma in William Styron's (1951/1992) *Lie Down in Darkness.* The novel opens with Milton Loftis waiting at a train station in Port Warwick, Virginia, for the return of his daughter's body from New York after her suicide. Before Styron situates us in the suffering of a father shattered by his daughter's death, however, he uses second-person narration to provide us with a perspective on the landscape from the train window. The Southern landscape thus contains a radical loss and invites us to consider what in the landscape might bind its effects. As this pastoral account makes clear, the binding force is a projection of the white mind, an objectified and caricatured black man. Styron writes:

> Now the sun is up and you can see the mist lifting off the fields and in the middle of the fields the solitary cabins with their slim threads of smoke unwinding out of plastered chimneys and the faint glint of fire through an open door and, at a crossing, the sudden, swift tableau of a Negro and his hay-wagon and a lop-eared mule: the Negro with his mouth agape, exposing pink gums, staring at the speeding train until the smoke obscures him, too, from view, and the one dark-brown hand held cataleptic in the air. (p. 10)

These lines expose a violent psychosocial practice of using the landscape to secure racial difference, a practice evident throughout Southern literature and given theoretical support by the Southern Agrarians.

Suzanne Jones (2002), however, has begun to map a counter-movement in the discourse of the rural landscape. Despite the hegemony of the Southern Agrarians, she shows there have been significant interventions by contemporary white writers. She accounts specifically for the work of Madison Smartt Bell and Ellen Douglas, white writers who have attempted to work alongside black writers in their efforts to "reclaim this [Southern] landscape haunted by racism" (p. 122). These writers, Jones argues, use a Southern rural aesthetic to challenge white privilege and inequitable distribution of land in the South, evidencing the emergence of Southern Agrarians markedly different in perspective from their predecessors. "The enemies of the contemporary southern agrarians," Jones optimistically writes, "are no longer specialization and mechanization but racism and self-deception." They attempt, she continues, to undermine a "regionalism of the mind" that "homogenizes the South and its people" (p. 146).

This analysis of Southern place in literary history exposes a discourse that provides a sense of coherence to white masculinity as it is lived in the South. It connects the language of the landscape with an intransigent Southernness, and also suggests that this language is a potential medium for unsettling Southern nostalgia and reactionary race and gender politics. This tension represents an important feature of the process of creating and re-creating Southern regional identity that Gray (2000) calls "Southern self-fashioning." Gray explains that because of Southerners' varying and ambivalent attachments to Southern land there is "a slippage of meaning at work in regional self-identification" (p. 498). In *Southern Aberrations,* Gray captures various writers' difficult relationships with Southern place to reveal the complexity of the notion of Southernness. He elaborates on the South through "the writings of those who have viewed it aslant" (p. ix), emphasizing the historical instability of the vision of the Nashville Agrarians. "To be Southern could always mean many things," Gray explains, "despite the attempts of those like the Nashville Agrarians, who tried to align it with relatively specific notions of human culture and the body politic" (p. 498).

In the following chapters I explore the Agrarian perspective, interpreting literary works that both support and disrupt the alignment of conventional white masculinity and the rural aesthetic. I also conceptualize a curriculum that returns the tensions of cultural complexity—the "slippage of meaning" in regional identity—to the white patriarchal vision of the South exemplified in the Nashville Agrarians' work and legacy.

CHAPTER 2

Southern Place: Autochthony, White Masculinity, and Southern Aberrations

Introduction

Place is central to the study of the American South. The question of the meaning and power of place underpinned the earliest efforts to define and understand the region. And place remains a critical concept in an ongoing process of regional identification and inquiry. To draw on this tradition for a social-psychoanalytic curriculum, we must review the concept of place that it advances, tracing the political consequences of claiming Southern place as a subject position and source of expression.

Places are both internal and external. They can inspire thought and reflection; they can also palliate and deflect subjective and social conflicts that call for our attention. In this chapter, I show that place has been used in Southern literature and criticism to produce a narrative of domination that compensates for a psychological insufficiency experienced by white men. In the minds of the authors discussed here, Southern place is more than a mimetic representation of a real space captured in writing; it is an imaginary space and a symbolic concept that has served to promote certain beliefs and patterns in culture, emboldening white masculinity. This use of place forms a subliminal cultural rhetoric, a rhetoric that is rooted deep in a desire to confirm the coherence of self-presence in an otherwise chaotic, emergent world. Thus, place is not merely a physical dimension; it is also a psychic terrain, one that has already been tilled and cultivated by a broader myth and that can be examined in a range of discourses—from criticism, literature, and the arts to biography and autobiography.

In traditional Southern scholarship, place represents a determinative geography and an ingrained social texture. Traditional Southern critics trace the significance of place to the palpability of the visual external world and to a more nebulous though equally binding fabric of social norms and relationships (Romine, 2002). Within this formulation, the subjective dimension of place is reduced to the notion of a "sense of place," the measure of one's emotional orientation toward the world. The notion is reductive in my view because it marks a profound, if not always positive, sense of place as a defining and therefore universal characteristic of Southern identity, which excludes the subjectivities of others, women and blacks specifically, who experience place differently than white men.

Southern place has exuded a certain flavor of the real that has been popularized by culture and the arts, securing the normative myth of regional unity, rarely marked by the violence and subjugation that history unfolds. For example, when we view regionalist photography—such as a Walker Evans photograph of a barbershop in Atlanta or a William Eggleston photograph of deteriorating furniture in a yard in rural Mississippi—these images assure us of the actuality of place as they conjure up a concrete sense of being-in-the-world. But such an experience is narrowly explained in traditional Southern studies: one's capacity to grasp the presence, while believing in the ineffability, of these Southern "landscapes" signals the genuineness of place and the immutability of Southern identity. "Southern place," therefore, acts as a master signifier (Žižek, 1989, pp. 87–89). It grants identity to those who embrace it and totalizes the meaning of diverse cultural milieus and experiences, so much so that even images of social inequity and violence in the region can be incorporated within, and made to contribute to, a coherent sense of place. As Warren Zanes (1998) suggests, images of the South are often organized in a way that "exerts pressure" on the South's history of violence, emphasizing instead "the curious, lasting innocence and authenticity of Southern *community*" (p. 10, emphasis in original).

In his deconstruction of Southern place, Romine (2002) suggests that we know someone is Southern if his or her sense of place runs deep. This undertheorized but widely referenced Southern sense of place has significant consequences for autobiographical curriculum inquiry in the American South. By rooting Southern identity in an intense and unquestionable affective relationship to a relatively static conception of place, it presents an obstacle between subjectivity and the external world, impeding further inquiry into the complex social and historical construction of the self. In such a way, for the writers I discuss in this book, Southern place is mediated through and dominated by narratives that have preceded their birth, their own belated stories reiterating the stories of the previous generations. I now want to further describe the rhetoric that connects the land to the social realm in a monolithic conception of Southern place. Doing so will enable me, in later chapters, to unsettle this assumed coherence and return the disturbing questions of Southern place to a reconceptualized Southern subject.

In this chapter I focus on a central figure in the literature and politics of the American South. Donald Davidson's contribution to the Agrarian movement and his advocacy of a set of ideas about the South can serve as a template for understanding how intellectuals, in presenting theories of Southern culture and identity, may expose their own racist biases. Identity politics that focus exclusively on the heritage of a Southern tradition and fixate on the purity of the land exclude the meaningful presence of the corruption associated with the ownership and actual use of the land. Davidson's use of the land in his aesthetics and theory of regional identity promulgates a concept of racial difference that has serious implications not only for the scholar but also for future generations of educators. These educators will be confronting a student population of black Southerners who know by their very genealogies that there is nothing so ideal or uninterrupted about the Southern terrain; ownership of the land includes a shadowy history of the ownership of slaves who worked the land, a history that unconsciously pervades education while remaining inadequately addressed in the school curriculum.

Davidson held certain beliefs about the land that were disputed by his friends and colleagues, which made him particularly sensitive to the experience of displacement in his personal and professional life. His theory of Southern identity expresses this sensitivity, showing that he yearned for a more comprehensive model of Southernness, one that could distinguish the region from other parts of the country. In this chapter, I demonstrate more precisely how a sense of displacement and insecurity unsettles Davidson's vision of the South, positioning him both as an Agrarian and as a social critic. His ambivalence provides an interesting lens on the flaws of the Agrarian model, and it provides an explanation for why the monism of the Agrarian vision remains influential even as it has given way to more pluralistic views.

The Nashville Agrarians and the Autochthonous Ideal

Since the Civil War and Reconstruction, Southern white men have vehemently claimed literal ground in attempts to anchor themselves in consistent and untroubled subjectivity. This dynamic appears most prominently in the work of the Nashville Agrarians, the poets and critics who, from the 1930s, sought to define the South and Southern literature through a rural aesthetic and agrarian ethos. In the Agrarian manifesto *I'll Take My Stand* (1930/1977), the Twelve Southerners attack the culture of industrialism and call for the protection of the rural order of the South. Generally, the Agrarians advance a notion of an autochthonous Southern identity, claiming the authentic (white male) Southerner derives his being from the land and lives in harmony with society and culture. Southern places, in their formulation, "[exert] a distinctive valence such that perceptions, attitudes, and representations [emerge] in a predictable, normative, and 'natural' way" (Romine, 2002, p. 30).

In *I'll Take My Stand,* John Crowe Ransom (1930/1977), a leading figure in the Agrarian movement, leaves no doubt as to the location of the meaning of place. Ransom describes the yeoman farmer at work on the land, pointing to the ground, assuring us of the profound physical presence of Southern place:

> He [the farmer] identifies himself with a spot of ground, and this ground carries a good deal of meaning; it defines itself for him as nature. He will till it not too hurriedly and not too mechanically to observe in it the contingency and the infinitude of nature; and so his life acquires its philosophical and even its cosmic consciousness. (pp. 19–20)

For Ransom, intimacy with the land provides sublime access to the spirit of nature. Such closeness, the Nashville Agrarians argue, forms the core of the Southerner's identity.

In the writing of Donald Davidson (1930/1977), we discover another feature of the Agrarian ideology: rhetoric that binds social conditions to the physicality of the land. Here the palpable countryside not only provides passage into the vastness of nature and spirit, as Ransom suggests, but actually adumbrates the essence of Southern values, private and public. Davidson theorizes Southern identity through the figure of the artist: "[T]he provincial artist ought to enjoy special blessings. More nearly than his big-city colleague, he should be able to approximate a harmonious relation between artist and environment. Especially to his advantage is his nearness to nature in the physical sense. . . . [N]ature is an eternal balancing factor in his art, a presence neither wholly benign, nor wholly hostile" (pp. 57–58). As a "balancing factor," Davidson argues, nature prevents one from becoming "in the narrow sense an artist 'of the soil,' dealing [merely] in the picturesque" (p. 57). As Washington Irving believed, nature belongs to a more consequential art. The "real importance [of art] in life," Davidson explains, "is as a significant and beautiful way of shaping whatever there is to be shaped in life, secular and religious, private and public" (p. 56). Drawing on his contact with land and nature, the Southerner "cultivate[s] a historical consciousness that permeates manners, localities, institutions, the very words and cadence of social intercourse" (p. 53).

Davidson's conviction is upheld in the cultural and artistic forms of engagement practiced by many Southern writers and artists, producing and proliferating a narrative myth; however, as I will show in later chapters, black Southern writers ironically traverse this mythical landscape, penetrating the white psyche and reclaiming the images of black men and women that have been reduced to stereotypes. Thus one of the questions that guides my exploration into the permutations of Southern identity is: what does this vision of place make of the black individual whose relationship to the land has been one of burden and who has not shared in the culture of power—for whom history is a continuous weight of agony, separation, and oppression? Denied the "social intercourse" of white privilege, black men and women, in the white mind and the discourse of regional identity, become the abject of Southern place. Davidson makes this exclusionary force clear, writing obstinately in response to John Dollard's (1937) *Caste and Class in a Southern Town* that the South "will not support a program of improvement which implies a change of [racial] status." At stake, he continues, are "self-preservation and pride of race and tradition" (quoted in King, 1980, p. 60).

Like Ransom, Davidson moves from the particularity of the land to an argument about its broader significance. However, rather than claiming, simply, a merger with nature's aura, he claims that nature controls social relations. Through references to religion, family, and social institutions, Davidson defines a social terrain that serves as a refuge from social contingency and the threat of racial integration, a refuge that borrows its legitimacy from the concreteness of the land.

As a Nashville Agrarian, Davidson upholds an "autochthonous ideal," a form of consciousness that, he claims, enables Southernness to issue forth from nature. The autochthonous ideal is "a condition," Fred Hobson (1991) explains, "in which the writer [is] in a certain harmony with his social and cultural environments, [is] nearly unconscious of it as a 'special' environment, quaint or rustic or backward, and thus [is] not motivated by any urge to interpret or explain" (p. 80). Like High Romanticism, which bordered precariously on a regressive form of primitivism, the Agrarian model is one that resists technological advance and progress, preferring a more idyllic vision of a blended, perhaps ineffable, but primary, relation between a sentient mind and insentient nature. Along with this extremely influential conception of natural Southern emergence, Davidson conceptualized, more than any of his Agrarian colleagues, the social-cultural terrain of Southernness, insisting that Southerners are held together by a "folk-chain" of collective memory. Here we must acknowledge that when one conceives of one's self as "heterogeneous," or the result of multiple overlappings of the same, previous, and subsequent generations, collective memory can serve as a model of compassionate remembering and possible intervention. However, one must keep some distance from the past to avoid the inheritance of a hatred that reactivates trauma and continues the cycle of violence. Davidson, we will see, was unable to find that distance.

The medium of Southern tradition and identity, Davidson explains, imparts "*who we are, where we are, where we belong, what we live by, what we live for*" (emphasis in original; quoted in Murphy, 2001, p. 92). In "The Center That Holds"—an essay written for the journal *Southern Partisan*—Davidson further elaborates, "What passes from memory to memory, without benefit of the historian's record, is as old in time as the memories that it expresses, and if it is accepted it endures as long as the land and people that accept it" (quoted in Murphy, 2001, p. 92). Authentic Southern values and relationships emanate from the vivid and palpable landscape. Resisting representation (in "the historian's record"), they can be apprehended only as texture and through a uniquely Southern "sense of place."

By avoiding historicity in the South, an intellectual such as Davidson is able to deny the culpability of the white race in slavery and racial subjugation. By relegating all history and perception to a visionary model of harmony, he conveniently avoids taking a measure of his own being against the violence of the past, avoiding as well the past's irreparable brokenness. The South's racist history, then, does not serve Davidson as context for self-understanding; it does, however, return from this repression in his conceptualization of place. In "Still Rebels, Still Yankees"—an essay Richard King (1980) calls "an otherwise bucolic evocation of rural Georgia and Jeffersonian virtue" (p. 60)—Davidson dismisses the lynching of black men, a practice that plagued the South and the nation for over a century (Pinar, 2001). Exposing the racist core of his theory of Southern place, Davidson writes: "What did a few lynchings count in the balance against the continued forbearance and solicitude that the Georgian felt he exercised toward these amiable children of cannibals" (quoted in King, 1980, p. 60).

Understood in terms of the autochthonous ideal, place explains if not justifies the race, class, and gender inequities as well as the violence of Southern history. The traditional conception of place reifies social hierarchies; that is, it enables the perception of social hierarchies as innate characteristics of a place, reducing place—a complex subjective and social category of understanding—to a stabilizing binary of physical presence and social law. "Traditionally, 'place' has signified a nexus of is and ought," Romine (2002) explains, "a describable outside metonymically associated with a network of imperatives, codes, norms, limitations, duties, obligations, and relationships" (p. 24). Though this binary is most prominent in the work of the Nashville Agrarians, whose "implicit agenda" Susan Donaldson (1997) argues, was "to protect and consolidate the masculinity of the white male southern writer" (p. 505), the binary persists even in much criticism directed against social injustice and white male cultural hegemony in the American South. It is such unconscious repetitions of racist and sexist history that a social-psychoanalytic curriculum can help us work through.

I now return to Davidson's life and work to reveal more specifically how place has functioned as a projection and protective harbor for the white male subject in a state of identity crisis. Having already discussed how Davidson's argument for the meaning of Southern place is rooted in a racist politics and relies on an eschatological vision of white hierarchy, I turn to a more specific discussion of the personal foundations of Davidson's "identity politics."

Donald Davidson's Marshallville: An Instance of Identity Politics

The people [are] a great deal like the land.

—Donald Davidson (1938, p. 137)

In 1933, on Confederate Memorial Day, Donald Davidson—a Vanderbilt University English professor and poet—addressed a gathering in Marshallville, Georgia, concerning the agrarian South's embodiment of cultural value. Marshallville had become for Davidson a refuge from personal and professional turmoil he was experiencing at Vanderbilt, and therefore substantiated his particular vision of the harmony that could be achieved between an individual and his community. Davidson's speech to the town mirrored the community values he witnessed there, and he presented these values as the foundations of a worthy existence. Believing such existence to be intimately connected with the land and agrarian life, Davidson ultimately condemned "the ideal of a tightly unified, urban, industrial nation" and praised a "spiritual secession" from "mechanized America" (quoted in Murphy, 2001, p. 99). Though he argued that such a movement against the industrial state was developing in regions throughout the nation, he insisted the movement's spirit was essentially Southern. For Davidson, the virtuousness of the Southerner issued from his particular relationship to the land.

Davidson sought to define and protect the rural order of the South, an order threatened at every turn, he and his Agrarian colleagues believed, by the culture of industrialism.[8] Davidson found renewed inspiration for the Agrarian cultural project in the sense of harmony and cohesion he experienced in Marshallville. Participating in community affairs, singing with the local chorus, and speaking to discussion groups, Davidson made of his experience in Marshallville a bulwark against the storm of problems he faced in Nashville. In Michael O'Brien's (1979) account of Davidson's mindset, "Marshallville gave one precious commodity to a man deep in self-doubt—respect" (p. 194).

Davidson sought respect in the face of professional discord and personal tragedy. His "academic career was fraught with insecurity and hardship, which . . . fostered and compounded an ever present defensiveness" (Murphy, 2001, p. 95). Davidson's colleagues, Allen Tate and John Crowe Ransom specifically, became irritated with his wavering on the question of agrarianism as a "practical" program of land management. As they questioned Davidson's competency, they distanced themselves from him emotionally. And the distance between a beleaguered Davidson and his friends "had a striking simultaneity with his shift towards a more literal sectionalism" (O'Brien, 1979, p. 190).

Early in 1932, the campus dormitory in which Davidson and his family lived burned to the ground. They lost most of their possessions, including diaries, correspondence, and poetry Davidson published as a member of the Fugitives, the Vanderbilt group from which the Agrarians emerged. After the tragedy, another of the Twelve Southerners, John Donald Wade, gave Davidson his home in Marshallville for the year (Murphy, 2001, p. 96).

Throughout his time in Marshallville, Davidson corresponded with Wade and a few other colleagues at Vanderbilt. In Davidson's letters, Marshallville appears as an agrarian ideal. Marshallville puts Davidson, he writes, "in good humor and good courage" (quoted in Smith, 2003, p. 64). Moreover, it becomes a muse and object of veneration. Writing about the Memorial Day speech, Davidson explains: "I tried hard to make it my best possible effort—my utmost best being, in my opinion, far below what Marshallville deserves" (quoted in Smith, 2003, pp. 50–51). Davidson frequently refers to Marshallville as Eden, and when he is away from this Georgia sanctuary, he longs for "the Spirits of the Place" (p. 92).

Davidson's detailed accounts of the Marshallville landscape reveal the way his psychological ease is a fabric woven through pastoral images. In November of 1932, he writes to Wade: "The garden is growing, trees keep their leaves . . . I am nibbling my pen, time goes smooth on, all is well" (quoted in Smith, 2003, p. 32). With thoughts of his collegial conflicts at Vanderbilt, that "smoking cauldron of Nashville," Davidson asks Wade to speak of him to his colleagues. He wants Wade to tell them "something poetic and grand," that he is "a sort of fortunate Lazarus dwelling in Abraham's bosom" (p. 24). He continues: "Let them picture me sucking a stalk of sugar cane, under a pecan tree, reciting, under these extraordinarily spacious Georgia skies where swallows and night-hawks crowd the evening air, the Southern equivalent of Om Mane Padme Om" (p. 24).

In a letter to Andrew Lytle, Davidson shows that inextricable from his apprehension of the rural landscape and agrarian life is a deep nostalgia for the Old South and a desire to maintain a strict racial hierarchy:

> Marshallville is a grand place to rusticate . . . I lead a quiet life—cultivate a garden, wander about, read and (I hope) write, enjoy the people and the landscape. This is a really agrarian section—quite the Old South in tone and in deed. There are horses, mules, wagons, negroes, plantations, good soil, good people, good manners . . . I like it all tremendously. (Quoted in O'Brien, 1979, p. 194)

In these letters, whereas Marshallville is Edenic in character, Nashville is estranging. Nashville, Davidson writes, is a place of "litter and doom." "It is a lost city," he warns, "which I think the lord has hardly made up his mind to save. I do not want to perish with it" (quoted in Smith, 2003, p. 64). Davidson associates his alienation in Nashville more specifically with a particular kind of intellectual labor. In Nashville, his reading is "heavy—too heavy—sociology, geography, political theory" (quoted in Smith, 2003, p. 89). He thus yearns to be away from these abstractions, to be in Marshallville, "where people are people and things are things—not figures in a book" (quoted in Smith, 2003, p. 89).

Marshallville provided Davidson, he believed, with an unmediated relationship to Southern identity. Thus, as he spoke to the community of Marshallville, those who represented his confirmed image of authentic Southernness, Davidson defended his time in the town as a fertile withdrawal from the dangers of urbanization. "The good life," he explained, "is not to be found at too great a distance from the land, or apart from the intimate fellowship of kinfolks and friends, the mutual graciousness of family life, the solace of steadfast religious faith, and above all, the sense of belonging somewhere in a world which at best is changeable and insecure" (quoted in Murphy, 2001, p. 99).

This statement of the proper foundations of Southern identity captures the Agrarian ethos that Davidson, unlike his colleagues, would embrace throughout his lifetime. For Davidson, Agrarianism promoted a strict localism, and thereby differentiated regional identities. As we can see in his letters, for Davidson Agrarianism was not only an economic program; it was a theory of the proper relationship between subjectivity and community. As Paul Murphy (2001) argues, "Agrarianism became for him a form of white southern identity politics" (p. 7).

Davidson's Southern regionalism was "an intensely personal intellectual faith" that set him apart from his Agrarian colleagues, but it also exposed the influential and racist cultural politics at the foundation of the entire Agrarian movement (Murphy, 2001, p. 97). Since the publication of *I'll Take My Stand,* theorists of literature, regional culture, and social-political thought have shown that the Agrarianism of the Twelve Southerners was more variegated than the group's overall intransigence on the subject of modern industrialism once suggested. As I've indicated, Davidson straddled a particular rift in Agrarian criticism concerning the practical politics of the movement; a look at his shifting stance further illuminates his politics of place.

A major point of contention in Agrarian criticism has been whether Agrarianism should be interpreted as a metaphor for social and aesthetic values or as a practical economic program. In the early 1930s, Davidson did support a practical program of proprietary land management; that is, with the other Twelve Southerners, he called for the spread of subsistence farming to protect Southern place and culture. In the late 1930s, however, as his colleagues turned away from the Agrarian project, Davidson began to downplay practical economics and to emphasize the cultural principles of Agrarian thought (Bone, 2005, pp. 16–17). For Davidson, it seemed, farms were no longer necessary to perpetuate the Southern tradition.[9] However, if a shift in Davidson's thought had taken place, it was not clear when, thirty years later, he objected to Louis Rubin's account of Agrarianism in the introduction to the 1962 edition of *I'll Take My Stand.* In that essay, Rubin (1977) describes Nashville Agrarianism as "an extended metaphor, of which the image of the agrarian community is the figure, standing for and embodying . . . modern society" (p. xxviii). In the mid-1960s, then, seeming to revert to an older stance, Davidson resisted Rubin's aestheticized and humanistic interpretation of the Agrarian movement; he did so, Davidson argued, because if Agrarianism is only a metaphor, "you don't have to believe it at all" (quoted in Rubin, 1977, p. xvii). Securing belief in Southern place and culture was indeed Davidson's primary concern. If he seemed to embrace both sides of this argument, he did so, out of political convenience, to advance a politics neither side fully articulated.

Refusing to surrender the concreteness of the land to either the abstractions of modern sociology or a depoliticized, inconsequential art, Davidson, a poet, sought to create a poetics of the land that would secure and bequeath Southern identity and tradition. His political project was to control the meaning of the land in the formation of culture and society. This fact supports Murphy's (2001) argument that, among the Agrarians, it was Davidson's "ideas and instincts that were most predictive of future trends in the South and the nation" (p. 8). "Ironically, it is Davidson," Murphy continues, "the most reactionary of the original Agrarians, who is, in many ways, the most relevant of the Agrarians to contemporary concerns. He was a harbinger of identity politics, the Agrarian for whom history and heritage formed the core of personal meaning and self-esteem" (p. 8). Though Southern critics such as Hobson (1991) have tried to borrow Davidson's aesthetics of place and identity while distancing themselves from his politics, we must remember that these aesthetics support a fantasy of a unified South that enacts racial violence in the name of stable community. Davidson (1957) himself reveals this violence as he writes: "The South knows that it could not maintain its society in the desired equilibrium unless the alien element, now vastly enlarged, could be strictly controlled. And if it could not maintain the equilibrium, it could not maintain democracy for white people" (p. 209). To understand the cultural power of Davidson's aesthetics of place better, and to make this vision of place amenable to social psychoanalysis, I now turn to the work of contemporary critic W. J. T. Mitchell.

Idolatry of the Landscape

Bringing the tools of Lacanian psychoanalysis to the study of place, Mitchell (2002a) invites us to consider how the Imaginary dimension of the landscape becomes a force of cultural power. Landscape, in his formulation, is the phenomenon of place that frames our contact with elusive aspects of experience.[10] "Landscape exerts a subtle power over people," he writes, "eliciting a broad range of emotions and meanings that may be difficult to specify" (p. vii). Although these inexpressible experiences of landscape potentially disturb us, the landscape, as a gestalt, Mitchell argues, has the power to contain the disturbance. In other words, landscapes move us into a state characterized by an "indeterminacy of affect" and then stabilize or bind the effect of this indeterminacy. Mitchell explains: "As the background within which a figure, form, or narrative act emerges, landscape exerts the passive force of setting, scene, and sight" (p. vii). A landscape, then, can act as a depersonalized primal fantasy, confronting the subject with its own evanescence while providing the ego a sense of permanence. In fact, by aligning it with the Lacanian Imaginary, Mitchell posits the landscape as a correlate of our bodily ego, the aspect of place from which we either derive a sense of security or feel the threat of a rival. Mitchell (2002b), therefore, asks us to "think of landscape, not as an object to be seen or a text to be read, but as a process by which social and subjective identities are formed" (p. 1). This treatment of landscape can help us better understand the cultural power embedded in the Agrarians' autochthonous ideal.

To ineffable experiences of land and landscape, the Agrarians applied the notion of a Southern "sense of place," attempting to secure belief in the power of our surroundings to determine social relations.[11] Davidson explicitly counterposed this "sense of place" to other forms of social and cultural representation—those, for example, that appeared in the work of the sociologist Arthur Raper, who courageously exposed racial inequities and criticized racial violence in the South. "For Davidson and the Agrarians generally," Romine (2002) explains, "scientific representation of the South amounted to, in effect, an apostasy against their theory of mythic emergence" (pp. 29–30). The Agrarians claimed they were not constructing a Southern myth but "registering the spontaneous emergence of myth from a specific way of life" (p. 30). The meaning and power of Southern place are innate, the Agrarians argued, and they should be approached through the ways of life that emerge from a society structured around agrarian labor. The Twelve Southerners claimed the land in the name of virtuous living; we can see they in fact constructed a landscape of cultural power, which would leave the black person in a static and inferior position, both in terms of labor and in social life. They did so by vehemently defending the concrete world they saw over the theoretical abstractions that disrupted their vision of the world. In their "statement of principles," the Twelve Southerners (1930/1977) explain that authentic Southern culture, and thus the fundamental meaning of Southern place, is not "soft material poured in from the top" but rather "deeply founded in the way of life itself—in its tables, chairs, portraits, festivals, laws, [and] marriage customs" (p. xliv). This kind of psychological valence, the concretization of identity in the things of place, we see again in Chapter 3; however, there it is activated in the black writer's mind, disclosing an effort to disarticulate the bodily ideal conveyed through white masculinity, and an effort to reconstruct the space of desire.

Mitchell (2002c) warns that we should not take the emotional force of the landscape as simple evidence of the meaningfulness of place: "While it is important . . . to retrieve the memories and excavate the depths of landscape, one must register as well the sense in which landscape is all about forgetting, about getting away from the real in ways that may produce astonishing dislocations" (p. 263). The Nashville Agrarians mobilized the emotive and evocative power of landscape, natural and cultural, in support of the white patriarchal South. And their fascination with Southern land bred what Mitchell calls the "idolatry of the landscape" (p. 264). However, in idolizing the land, treating it as an inflated figure of worship, they veiled another inexpressible concern, a fear that white masculinity might be shattered by the race and gender antagonism on which it is founded. The power of this perceived crisis becomes clearer when it is viewed through a psychoanalytic account of hegemonic white masculinity. Before returning to the Agrarians and exploring the narratives of black and women writers who unsettle the Agrarian vision of place, in the next section I review what psychoanalysis can teach us about the identity crisis experienced by white men.

The Dominant Fiction and White Masculinity's Anxiety of Insufficiency

As I outlined in the "Introduction," Silverman (1992) posits the "dominant fiction" as an ideological belief system that is constituted through fantasy and solicits faith in the adequacy of the male subject, the unity of the Oedipal family, and the coherence of the patriarchal world. This psychosocial concept relies on Lacan's theory of the subject, in which subjectivity is formed as lack—as a void of being or absence of self—whereas the ego "fills the void at the center of subjectivity with an illusory plenitude" (p. 5). The ego, according to Lacan, arises from, a mirror function, an imaginary identification with an ideal ego, and "captates" the subject.[12] Silverman's notion of the dominant fiction accounts for a "collective mirror" that provides imaginary unity to society as a whole. Following Althusser, Silverman writes: "[S]ocial consensus is not a matter of rational agreement, but of imaginary affirmation," an affirmation "synonymous with the very constitution of the subject" (p. 24). We can think of the dominant fiction, therefore, as a collective ideal ego, a point of identification that provides self and society with imaginary coherence. Silverman continues, "Hegemony hinges upon identification; it comes into play when all the members of a collectivity see themselves in the same reflecting surface" (p. 24).

Seeing oneself in the collective mirror of the dominant fiction requires belief in the unity of the white male subject. That is, the dominant fiction negates knowledge of the white male subject's constitutive lack or castration in language. Because this "ideology is central to the maintenance of classic masculinity," Silverman (1992) argues, "the affirmation of classic masculinity is equally central to the maintenance of our governing 'reality'" (p. 16). Affirming the power of Southern white men, in other words, becomes necessary for maintaining the South's traditional "sense of place." Silverman's incisive analysis, however, opens the way for affirming white male subjectivity in its inevitable deviation from the cultural norm, while also suggesting why such deviations are felt as a threat.

"While white masculinity constitutes a hegemonic force in contemporary social, political, and economic domains," Thomas DiPiero (2002) explains, "we need to analyze it as a symptomatic reply to cultural demands, not as a self-generating ahistorical entity somehow able to endlessly reproduce itself" (p. 3). Following Silverman, DiPiero calls for the analysis of white masculinity as it is lived by white men. He differentiates such analysis from studies that conflate white male subjectivity and a white male cultural ideal. To understand how white male cultural power becomes reinstated historically, DiPiero would have us acknowledge "two extremes of white masculinity, neither of which is for any practical purposes readily available to us: on the one hand is the figure of hegemonic stability to which all other forms of identity are explicitly or implicitly compared; and on the other hand there is the identity as it is lived by real human beings" (p. 3). Hegemonic white masculinity, then, is the product of efforts to live "models of impossible identification" (p. 3). The disturbances and digressions that arise as white men negotiate these models, including those we've seen in Davidson's biography, are symptoms of a racist and sexist society; however, as such, they might be resymbolized in a social-psychoanalytic curriculum dedicated to unsettling the relationship between white masculinity and the public sphere.

Deviations from the cultural ideal of white masculinity, DiPiero (2002) argues, produce an "anxiety of insufficiency" in white men (p. 9). Much more than a personal affair, this anxiety draws on and expresses social conflict; it resonates with "antagonism" that occurs wherever "incompatible meanings or demands for response attempt to inhabit the same psychic, social, or economic space" (p. 42). DiPiero conceptualizes how this social antagonism is felt as "a disruption or a blockage in one's sense of identity" (p. 42). When alternative forms of masculinity are not well articulated and valued, white men perceive their failure to attain the hegemonic ideal as an external threat to their intimate core.[13] This threat, DiPiero argues, gives rise to a form of hysteria in conventional white men, characterized by "the projection of and consequent identification with a lack in the other" (p. 197).

This ongoing identity crisis in the lives of white men, I want to suggest, compels the white male Southerner's idolatry of the landscape. As a symbol of white masculinity, the land assuages the failure of the white male subject to occupy its projected ideal. The land has served Southern white men as a screen of fantasy. Their embrace of the land, a de-sexualized figure of homosocial bonding, has helped them defend against a sense of insufficiency and project that insufficiency onto women and black men.

Toward Alternative Phenomenologies of Southern Place

We have learned, thus far, that place is a crucial but overdetermined category of analysis in Southern studies. It is the primary trope in a process of regional self-identification that developed out of the efforts of white Southerners to protect the order of a violently racist society and became reinforced when those efforts dramatically and violently failed. White patriarchal culture in the American South became "The South" through the deeply felt losses of the Civil War and Reconstruction, and place became a narrative fetish assuaging the pain of this traumatic past (Smith, 2002). In the dominant culture of the region, therefore, place simulates soundness of identity and community around an anxiety of insufficiency. This version of place precludes reflection on the traumas of Southern history and thus obscures the question of the common good, a good that would be available not only to Southern white men but also to women and blacks.

On some level, the Southern male hegemonist knows that place, historically, is not solely the result of white efforts, that the land in fact exists as it does as the result of the labor of slaves forced to work on the land. Trying to reduce it to a simple correlative that can be taken back to a purer state, before its labored cultivation, Davidson and others act out a wish to cover the guilt of the region's history. Allen Tate, for example, expresses the burden of ambivalence about Southern identity. For Tate, Southern place compels a "backward glance" to Southern history but installs a deep sense of alienation from the region's supposedly intact spiritual past. Tate also explicitly communicates a "sense of defeat" inherited by white Southern men. In a letter to his friend John Gould Fletcher, Tate writes: "[O]ur self-knowledge has been forced on us at the point of bayonets that now rust in museums" (quoted in Murphy, 2001, p. 39). Thus, with a "backward glance" to white male trauma, Tate brings the dose of alienation necessary to fortify the Agrarians' collective project of whitewashing and aestheticizing Southern place, community, and history.

Davidson, on the other hand, as I have already discussed, seeks solace in Southern place and history. A devout adherent to Lost Cause mythology, Davidson believes the turn to Southern history does not alienate the authentic Southerner, but rather connects him with the collective memory and common identity of his white Southern brethren, reducing black men and women to figures in the landscape. Davidson had faith in an "obdurate and romantic immersion in southern culture," a frankly racist and patriarchal conception of the region (Murphy, 2001, p. 31). He argued that the arts will prevail only in societies that are "stable, religious, and agrarian," and that in the modern world, it is the South that produces the culture "where men [are] never too far removed from nature to forget that the chief subject of art, in the final sense, is nature" (p. 29). Although Davidson resisted Tate's pessimism about the excavation of Southern history, his life and writing also represent the conditions of beleaguered white male subjectivity. In his case, however, the palliative is an overdetermined conception of place.

Thus, women and black Southerners would have to interrupt and unsettle the white patriarchal conception of place found in the writings of the Agrarians and other white male writers for their voices to be heard (Henninger, 2004; Yaeger, 2000). Challenging the conception of a universal "sense of place" in the South, they have articulated narratives that more accurately reflect the cultural and political complexity of the region. Though traditional ideas about Southern place remain influential, feminist, critical race, and postcolonial theories currently pose a substantial challenge to their function within Southern studies (McPherson, 2003; Jones & Monteith, 2002). Many contemporary scholars of the American South have heeded critiques of regionalism and conceptions of the local to theorize culturally and historically dynamic rather than static and unitary Southern places (Henninger, 2004; Ladd, 2002). This contemporary work unsettles the relationship between the two domains traditionally understood to constitute place: the "describable outside" and the "[social] network of imperatives, codes, norms, limitations, duties, obligations, and relationships" (Romine, 2002, pp. 23–24). It therefore enables new mappings of race and gender in the region.

An example of this more complex view of place is Yaeger's (2000) study of Southern women's writing, *Dirt and Desire.* Yaeger challenges the "virtues of rootedness" so prevalent in Southern literature and criticism to uncover other subjective and social dimensions of Southern place, those that have emerged through the denial of histories of racial violence and oppression (p. 14). Whereas Davidson claimed for Southerners an autochthonous relationship to the land, Yaeger insists we think of Southern places in terms of a "reverse autochthony." Yaeger uses this notion to account for a disturbing metaphorical pattern in Southern women's writing, one that parallels real acts of physical and social violence. Repeatedly the writers Yaeger examines describe places where "African American women and men [have been] flung to the earth" (p. 16). They are not settled or in harmony with the earth, but, in fact, fed to it, as if they were disposable bodies. African Americans, in the white racist mind, are undifferentiated from the tactile earth, and are therefore so submerged within its substance, or violated by it, that they are not distinguishable from it. And yet they lay the ground for Davidson's Agrarian myth of self-consummatory powers in the South. They become human debris, discarded to purify the space of white patriarchy. Yaeger cites Zora Neale Hurston's *Their Eyes Were Watching God* to reveal this psychosocial pattern, the violent intermingling of black bodies and the land. In the novel, Hurston describes the consequences of a hurricane that hits Lake Okeechobee. She writes: "[C]orpses were not just found in wrecked houses. They were under houses, tangled in shrubbery, floating in water, hanging in trees, drifting under wreckage" (quoted in Yaeger, 2000, p. 16). Yaeger argues that this and other literary depictions of "throwaway bodies" mark the historical conditions of African Americans in the South, writing of

> women and men whose bodily harm does not matter enough to be registered or repressed—who are not symbolically central, who are looked over, looked through, who

> become a matter of public and private indifference—neither important enough to be disavowed nor part of white southern culture's dominant emotional economy. (p. 68)

Thinking of place through the notion of reverse autochthony, Yaeger refuses the romantic notion of harmony and connectivity between self and Southern place, and she asks us to confront the South as a site where men and women have been "hurled into water or earth without proper rituals, without bearing witness to grief, without proper mourning" (p. 17).

Yaeger (2000) asks that we find "maps for tracing alternative phenomenologies of place," maps that might inspire "ways for redistricting a southern social geography" (p. 22). In Chapters 3 and 4, I participate in this project by turning to the writing of Reginald McKnight, Randall Kenan, Yusef Komunyakaa, and Ellen Douglas—black and women writers who explore the psychical underside of the traditional South. Like Yaeger, other scholars of the South have worked to understand the complex subjective and social vectors of place. In increasingly progressive ways, new conceptualizations of place frame the analysis of Southern literature (Jones & Monteith, 2002; Kreyling, 1998), history (Hale, 1998), cultural identity (McPherson, 2003), and political thought (Bone, 2003, 2005; Dunbar, 2004; Murphy, 2001). And studies of Southern place in the field of education have significantly framed a curriculum of social psychoanalysis for the region (Edgerton, 1996; Kincheloe & Pinar, 1991; Pinar, 2001; Perez, Fain, & Slater, 2004; Slattery & Daigle, 1994; Whitlock, 2007). However, as my description of a white male identity crisis suggests, the unsettling of hegemonic conditions can compel their refortification. This fact calls for our attention to an ongoing crisis of Southern place.

The Crisis of Place in the American South

Romine (2002) argues that the traditional conception of place survives in contemporary Southern studies despite, and perhaps because of, the manifestation of a significant "crisis of place" in Southern literature and criticism (p. 24). The current crisis of place, Romine suggests, has two causes. The first is that (post)modern society has transformed Southern locales into less conspicuously Southern places. The second is that contemporary critical theory challenges assumptions about the representation of place. That is, the idea of place as a narrative or discursive construct undermines the traditional idea that place is determinative and available for mimetic representation.

However these challenges have unsettled place, Romine (2002) explains, "traditional concepts of place are still salient enough that deviations from them can be recuperated as markers of Southern literary identity; a kind of discontinuous continuity exists even if place isn't what (or even where) it used to be" (p. 26). In fact, this challenge to the coherence of Southern place has historical antecedents that suggest a pronounced crisis of place is fundamental to the traditional cultural work of defining the region. Romine recalls that in the 1930s, when Tate described the flourishing of Southern letters in terms of a "conscious[ness] of the past in the present," he did so to account for an artistic mindset born of alienation, one threatened by industrial growth and a loss of religious coherence in the region (quoted in Romine, 2002, p. 26). Romine states this point more broadly, emphasizing a crucial dynamic at the foundation of traditional conceptions of Southern place: "It may prove that an overdeveloped eschatological sense is one of the more enduring characteristics of the southern literary tradition: the southernness of place, it seems, is always in danger of expiring" (p. 26). This threat to place is something to be resisted, refuted, and rejected if one's investment in self-presence depends on the values that Davidson promotes. For the Agrarians, it founded an eschatology that sanctioned the position of the master, and even gave mastery a preordained destiny. As I've shown, however, within this position of supposed mastery, one can always find disturbances and digressions.

In *Southern Aberrations,* Gray (2000) makes a similar argument about the crisis of place. "The South as a term of self-identification was, after all, born out of crisis; and the area known as Southern has remained almost continually in a critical state" (p. 372). Southern place gains its semblance of stability—its supposed innate and determinative value—through Southerners' recourse to a narrative about place being at risk. In later chapters, I explore this calamity—how texts depict the tensions between competing versions of the South.

One of the curious things about Davidson's position, and that of others who advance a monolithic vision of the South, is that it avoids the realities of place to the extent that it distorts it. A persistent difficulty with Southern place is the tension between the imaginary construct of a monolithic South and the cultural pluralism of the region. Gray (2000) situates his notion of Southern culture in this tension. The South, he explains, has always been composed of "a number of castes, classes, and smaller communities that at best live in uneasy coexistence with each other and at worst are in active conflict," although some "choose to claim that their South is the South, their story the master narrative" (p. 501). The tension between cultural plurality and regional definition infuses "the cultural work that has evolved ideas of the South and Southernness" (p. 501). Thus the practice of regional self-identification, Gray explains, "occurs in history, and is a result of the forces working in the field of historical evolution. But its end result is to transfix the beings, the objects of study, and leave them stamped with an inalienable, nonevolutive character—to sever them from the living tissue of their moment in time" (pp. 500–501). As we know from psychoanalysis, however, any act of severing place from history will confront elsewhere the history it defers.

The extensive literary analysis in Gray's (2000) *Southern Aberrations* contributes to our understanding that no South, no Southern place, exists settled in the soil and harmoniously intermingled with the landscape. To believe that is to obviate the fact of slavery and to continue to ignore the cultural contributions of blacks and women. Gray, therefore, emphasizes the difficulties in experiences with Southern place, illuminating a rich and diverse literary tradition and compelling deeper reflection on our lives in the region. He writes:

> A moment of special crisis, when the terms of our relations to things—which include, most crucially, our language—are brought into question, can force anyone to think more critically, argue more provocatively, and write with more imaginative force and daring than those living in more comfortable times. (p. 371)

As teachers and scholars of education in the American South, how can we commit ourselves to exploring the tensions, difficulties, and crises Southern place endows? How can we write through place, acknowledging a draw toward secure subjective emplacement, while working against the further alignment of place and cultural dominance? In the final section of this chapter, I provide a theoretical sketch of such a practice, one I pursue in the remaining chapters and interludes.

Working Through Southern Place

In his analysis of the landscape as idol, Mitchell (2002c) insists that "the critical exposure of idols to the light of historical analysis is rarely enough to disenchant or dethrone them" (p. 264). In other words, cogent persuasion alone cannot disabuse us of the embedded ideologies that damage our lives. "What is required," Mitchell explains, borrowing from the language of psychoanalysis, "is a working through of the idols" (p. 264). Mitchell's work inspires my return to the Agrarians and my autobiographical treatment of their aesthetic of Southern place. I return to work through the land as an idol of Southern culture. Mitchell dramatically expresses the potential of such a project. Quoting Nietzsche, he explains we work through the idols of the dominant culture by "striking them . . . with a 'hammer as with a tuning fork,' so as not to smash them, but to make them sound and resonate, divulge their own hollowness, and vomit up the human sacrifices they have demanded" (Mitchell, 2002c, p. 264).

Dean (1991) takes up this task where the American landscape has been idolized, suggesting how we might return more critically to our study of Southern place. Drawing on the poetry of Gary Snyder, Dean elaborates a theory of American culture that takes the land to be the primary figure of the American unconscious. Snyder, Dean shows, addresses and represents American culture in such a way that exposes the unconscious on which the hegemonic American subject is founded. This treatment of the American subject helps disclose the unconscious workings of the white male subject, who, in confluence with nature and in pursuit of a mastery of consciousness over nature, translates his subjectivity into poetic discourse. Dean argues the dominant conception of citizenship in the United States denies the influence of the land on the consciousness of the country's inhabitants. To the Europeans who in the fifteenth century discovered this already populated territory, the land was a figure of utter newness and support for a fantasy of unlimited opportunity. As the land became the material site of the deracination and genocide of American Indians, it remained a point of symbolic identification and began to serve European Americans in their erasure of the nation's violent history from consciousness. Dean writes,

> What we know as the United States came into being based on its destruction of the native inhabitants . . . and its expropriation of their home, the land. Because the European settlement of America began as a political and religious experiment intended to represent the pinnacle of civilisation and the morally best form of social organisation . . . the destruction upon which it was founded constitutes not just a paradox or a national embarrassment; rather, it constitutes something absolutely inadmissible to American consciousness. To be American, truly American, means not to know in a profound way the meaning of the United States's origins. (p. 2)

These origins of the United States include the repression of the nation's violent inception. Because the repression occurs through an attachment to the land, Dean argues, the American unconscious "consists of nothing other than a relation to the American ground itself" (p. 3). As my review of Agrarian writing and philosophy suggests, white men in the South—in the name of regional identity—have redoubled the repressive power of the land metaphor.

Dean discovers a social-psychoanalytic response in the work of Gary Snyder. Snyder's broken style attests to the inability of white men to truly meld the disparate aspects of the landscape and to convene them under one organized subjectivity, or one citizen. Through a focused analysis of Snyder's poetry, Dean develops the notion of "inhabiting the ground." Inhabiting the ground, for Dean, is a problem of decentering the self and relating anew to land and community in order to disrupt and potentially transform the cultural values (individualism, racial hierarchy, gendered oppression) that dominate life in America. Following Dean, I want to suggest that our relationships to land and landscape in the South, our perceptions of the environment broadly conceived, constitute a vague map of a cultural unconscious, a medium through which we might witness the exclusions and distortions that found hegemonic conceptions of regional identity.

AUTOBIOGRAPHICAL INTERLUDE

Questioning Homewardness

My effort to conceptualize a curriculum of Southern place dedicated to social justice takes me through traditional and progressive Southern studies and leads me to the analysis of contemporary Southern literature. But my study of place also taps a more personal project. Investigating the role of place in my self-formation, I have become more aware of the circumstances of my struggle to negotiate the boundary between home and the social world beyond it. The subject of place conjures up my sense of the protectiveness of home and the home seeking that subtends my efforts to voyage out. As I have studied place in art, literature, and theory, I have been reminded of the way I become entangled in a particular experience of home, drawn into the mystery of my origins and attached to a sense of connectedness and coherence my family once provided. This research helps me understand how my home has become magnified as a realm of meaning and how it reappears in the social and privates spaces I seek out. Moreover, it illuminates the personal and sociopolitical consequences of an unquestioned longing to inhabit places that support self and identity.

My research intertwines two projects, one largely social and the other personal. I am from the South. I have taught in my hometown of Baton Rouge, Louisiana, for ten years. I have explored the world through the textures of my home, while challenging my students and myself to interrogate the seduction of the familiar and the comfortable. Bringing my experience of home to my study of place in the American South, I find myself caught in a paradox. If my experience of home at times reflects the overdetermined sense of place that anchors hegemonic white masculinity in the South, it also contains the core of my concerns about self-analysis and social justice. If at times I've held a conception of home as an unmediated experience of place (Massey, 1994, p. 164), I can also recall experiences from my youth that taught me the "futility of that indispensable illusion," and that home is most productively grasped "not as the cell of family life" but as "the cutting edge that separates and binds public and private" (Bal, 2002, p. 193).

I interrogate place to broaden my conception of home, to bring into my bordered sense of subjectivity questions about the complex social terrain my students and I share. We currently share a terrain of reactionary politics, bequeathed to us through oppressive race and gender ideologies. I don't assume we experience these ideologies in the same way. And I don't assume they are uninterruptible. The lives of Southerners from Lillian Smith to Will Campbell, from Ida B. Wells to Yusef Komunyakaa, remind me that from particular social and subjective positions we can grapple with these ideologies and transform the practices of the reactionary South. However, I do understand these ideologies and practices to be embedded in our everyday lives in such a way that we become attached to them and therefore in such a way that makes it difficult to confront and move beyond them. This embedding happens in part through an overdetermined and undertheorized conception of place, a conception of place that continually surfaces in my autobiographical writing. The "working-through" that I depict in this research, therefore, is a personal and cultural process.

I teach with the intention of unsettling experiences we take for granted. This research unsettles my taken-for-granted experience of home, disclosing the way the dictates of home govern my sense of place. I discover how home travels with me. How the language and images of my homeplace can paradoxically obscure the circumstances of my upbringing, the sources of tension in my private life, and the politics of the geographical region I inhabit. And I discover the way home translates into a passionate attachment to place, a heightened expectation for stable ground and secure environs.

I understand the homewardness I've described to be a significant autobiographical and social-psychoanalytic problem. For when this version of place holds sway in society, as it has in the American South, we seek out places—forms of culture and community—that support the illusion of our fundamentally harmonious connection with the social world. We require places to redeem the disturbances of existence rather than learn to confront the social and subjective tensions they hold (Bersani, 1990). That Southerners continue to translate various and complex experiences of the South into a universal "sense of place" attests to the power of place to obscure the circumstances of our lives.

This research helps me understand the longing for secure place and the social and subjective conditions that nourish it. I want to locate in this longing the kernel of our subjective difference from the places we inhabit. If the longing for place registers a belief in the richness and plenitude of the external world, the effort to capture the meaning of place betrays a fundamental distance between the world and the self. In this distance lies intractable loss. But there too lies the provocation and possibility for us to engage with our surroundings without seeking to master them and the histories they bear. Surrendering this desire for mastery we open subjectivity and the world to new configurations.

CHAPTER 3

The Strange Limbo of Southern Place

He sat in some strange limbo, some odd place of ghosts and shadows, knowing he must rise.

—Randall Kenan (1992, p. 187)

Introduction

In the previous chapters, I showed how the dominant fiction in the South hinges on an image of the white male Southerner relating harmoniously with the land. This image is a symptom of collective belief in the adequacy of white masculinity and the coherence of Southern community. In other words, it symbolically links the authority of white men to the traditional conception of Southern place. In this formulation, Southern place determines individual and collective identity rather than unfolding from the desires and experiences of human beings as they relate to each other and their surroundings.

The traditional conception of place remains influential despite articulations of a "crisis of place" in the South. In fact, the claim that place is in a critical state can be read as an expression of doubt about the determinative ground of white patriarchy, one calling for the restoration of white patriarchal control. Black and women writers have significantly challenged white male claims to place and have opened a debate about what it means. Even so, many writers continue to draw on the traditional conception of place. It appears not only in conservative or reactionary texts but also in the writings of those who describe the South in its cultural diversity, including some who attempt to work through the region's traumatic past. But to justify claims to an innate Southern identity through a multicultural account of the region diminishes the experience of those the reactionary South has marginalized and oppressed. This leaves the social order and hegemonic white masculinity fundamentally unquestioned, even if it diversifies the map of the region.

Unlike contemporary Southern writers still attached to the traditional conception of place, Randall Kenan and Reginald McKnight unmoor us from the South's binding "sense of place" to compel our reconceptualization of the "ground" on which Southern place rests. Kenan and McKnight are black writers who represent the complexity of African American experience and identity as it relates to place. Both writers are trenchant in their depiction of the psychological entanglements of white male subjectivity. The two stories I turn to here—Kenan's "Run, Mourner, Run" and McKnight's "The White Boys"—take up and transform the Agrarian image of the white male subject in his relationship to land and landscape. In this way, Kenan and McKnight offer us a means for rethinking both Southern place and the construction of white male identity.

These authors expose unconscious dynamics of the hegemonic white male Southern subject. That is, through the eyes of the African American writer, the stories sardonically represent the white fantasies and gender dynamics that underlie the white male attachment to place as purifying ground. The short story "Run, Mourner, Run" engages the traditional Southern theme of the land, while suggesting the dominant perception of the land must disavow all interracial and homosexual relationships. This narrative depicts the protagonist's melancholic refusal to acknowledge how he is implicated in the region's racism and his own suffering. Yet, by delving into the (white male) South's repressed desires and identifications—this "odd place of ghosts and shadows" (Kenan, 1992, p. 187)—the narrative significantly refigures the Southern land as a vehicle for self-analysis and social understanding.

The novella "The White Boys" portrays the South in the absence of the markers of regional identity that palliate disturbing experiences of the region. This narrative boldly includes racial fantasies and disavowed gender attachments as constitutive of Southern place. In the absence of a sense of place to secure identity, we see that racial antagonism infuses the everyday experience of both blacks and whites and that in the face of this antagonism white men require women—wives and mothers—to protect them. The social picture becomes more and more disturbing and complex. Both "Run, Mourner, Run" and "The White Boys" also represent divisive relationships between white men as the precondition for the subjugation of black men. In different ways, therefore, they dissect white male subjectivity, exposing patterns of race and gender relations that contribute to the "strange limbo of Southern place."

Refiguring the Land: Randal Kenan's "Run, Mourner, Run"

"Run, Mourner, Run" centers on the theft of a piece of land and the relationships this injustice creates among a few citizens of the North Carolina town of Tims Creek. The land's rightful owner is Ray Brown, a prosperous black undertaker whose homosexuality is unknown to his wife and family. Ray's secret makes him vulnerable to a white landowner named Percy Terrell, who is obsessed with seizing the Browns' land and cleansing his imaginary landscape of those the white South has "flung to the earth" (Yaeger, 2000, p. 16). Intending to blackmail Ray for the land, Percy employs Dean Williams—a young, white, gay factory worker—to seduce Ray and therefore secure enough proof to expose his homosexuality. Speaking to Dean, Percy displays his avarice and racism. Moreover he reveals a frenzied desire that indicates the land's overdetermined significance for him. Percy says:

> They own a parcel of land I want. Over by Chitaqua Pond. In fact they own the land under Chitaqua Pond. I got them surrounded a hundred acres on one side, two hundred acres on one side, one fifty on the other. . . . They're blocking me. See? I want—I need that land. Niggers shouldn't own something as pretty as Chitaqua Pond. (Kenan, 1992, pp. 165–166)

There are two significant aspects of this confession, referring to the Southern land and its ownership. For Percy, the obstacle, the "block" to his sense of self, defined by how much land he can consider his pride, is Ray's ownership of the pond. It interrupts Percy's vision of white superiority and further identifies the land with the people who occupy it. If the degraded figure of the black man is situated on land considered "pretty," it devalues Percy's own property. Once the boundaries have been overreached, segregation has no meaning, leaving only the segregation that exists in Ray's paced work between the living and the dead. Ray and his family refer to this land as "homeplace." It represents the depths of their ancestry and the black community's resistance to white domination. It is a *place* that is *home*—something the uprooted slaves never had the option of owning or staying safely within. To Percy, however, it is a "passionate attachment" (Butler, 1997) through which he gains illusory control of the social order and his place in it, an attachment that conceals, as Judith Butler argues, disturbing aspects of the self, such as the homoerotic feelings in Percy's thoughts about the land, and about the men who occupy it.

In Kenan's depiction of Percy, he appropriates the figure of the white male Southerner in his unrealistic, and even obsessive, attachment to the land to conjure up and disrupt the dominant mythos of Southern place. Percy wants the land for no better reason than that the black man shouldn't have it; the black man's ownership of the land breaks up his sense of an imaginary continuity that is perpetuated in the landscape. Thus, Percy's attachment to the land signals Kenan's reworking of the agrarian metaphor by showing how unfounded, even absurd, the rights to property can be. Owning the land under the pond is of no real value; like the burden Ray "undertakes" in his work, it is about the remains of life, the underside or void. Percy accuses Ray of blocking him, but it is really Percy who is blocking Ray, as he tries *not* to see him, to void him from consciousness. With Percy's vehement pursuit of land, Kenan invites a closer reading of what is concealed in the attachment, and this gives us yet more insight into the Southern demand for rightful place as a means of identification and pride.

However, while it is Percy's relationship to the land that compels the events in the story, it is the protagonist, Dean Williams, a white male Southerner living at the margins of society, whose life reveals what white patriarchy can only attempt to disguise through its claim to place. Between the two white men, and in their relationship with Ray Brown, the land is a conduit of identifications and desires that conflict with the white men's avowed identities and social positions.[14] In fact, homosexuality, within the context of the story, is another blocked conduit for masculine idealization. Initially, it seems to Percy that to be homosexual is worse than being black; it carries a heavier social stigmatization. And yet, when the relationship between Dean and Ray deepens, we see that the seemingly distinct social stigmas are deeply entangled.

The story opens with a depiction of Dean sluggishly relating to the land. "Dean Williams sits in the tire," Kenan (1992) writes. "The tire hangs from a high fat sycamore branch. He swings back and forth, back and forth, so that air tickles his ears. His legs, now lanky and mannish, drag the ground" (p. 163). Dean swings listlessly and mournfully because, we discover later, he has betrayed Ray Brown—as well as his own desire for and identification with Ray—by helping Percy Terrell blackmail him. In this same setting, years before the betrayal, Dean related to the land differently. Dean's father had "hung the tire and hoisted a five-year-old Dean up by the waist and pushed him . . . higher and higher . . . until Dean, a little scared, could see beyond the old truck and out of over the field, his heart pounding" (p. 163). Dean's reminiscence indicates he once "had real dreams" (p. 164). But now Dean is bound by guilt, a guilt that is ubiquitous in the South, for betraying a black man for whom he felt affection. Unable to acknowledge the implications of his actions, he sits in the tire mournfully, "Swinging. Watching the last fingers of the late-October sun scratch at the horizon. Waiting. Looking at an early migration of geese heading south. Swinging" (p. 164).

Associating the land with Dean's lethargy and mournfulness, Kenan moves us toward the traumatic personal and collective histories embedded in it. He uses a language of the landscape, a poetics of the rural South, comparable to that of the Agrarians. For example, he describes Dean, "star[ing] off at the wood in the distance, over the soybean fields to the pine's green-bright, the oaks and the sycamores and the maples all burnt and brittle-colored" (p. 164). However, against the Agrarians' repressive poetics, Kenan recovers the land as more than pastoral hermitage; he recovers it, specifically, as a medium of complex sexual and cultural meanings.

To disrupt the traditional conception of Southern place, Kenan exposes the sexualized character of the land, something the Agrarians repressed, or refused to acknowledge. When Percy first approaches Dean about the blackmail, Dean believes Percy will make a sexual proposition. In other words, Dean takes Percy's desire for land *as* homosexual. Dean reflects that "it wouldn't have been the first time a grey-haired granddaddy has stopped his truck and invited Dean in" (Kenan, 1992, p. 165), suggesting what white heterosexual men claim not to know—that the trappings of conventional masculinity channel desire between men. As Percy approaches, Dean also recognizes his behavior as a breach of class boundaries. This heightens the sexual meanings of their encounter. To Percy, the wealthy landowner, "Dean was nothing more than poor white trash: a sweet-faced, dark-haired faggot with a broken down Ford Torino, living with his chain-smoking mama in a damn-near condemned house they didn't even own" (p. 166).

As Dean speculates about Percy's strange approach, he learns about Percy's lust for the land. Percy asks Dean to seduce Ray, again revealing the homoerotic nature of his racism and avarice: "I want you to get him for me. So to speak. . . . I want you to get to know him. Real good" (Kenan, 1992, pp. 165–166). Throughout their conversation, Dean attends to Percy's convoluted desires. And he recognizes Percy's greed and disdain for him. Dean nonetheless identifies with his racial power, because "before that day Percy had never said so much as 'piss' to Dean . . . [and] it was like an audience with the king to be picked up by ole Percy on the side of the road" (p. 166). In exchange for his aiding in the blackmail, Percy promises Dean a promotion and raise at the plant where he works. Dean agrees to the terms of the deal, solidifying the land as a figure of the homoerotic bond between these three men.

Caught in his identification with Percy, Dean pursues a sexual relationship with Ray. Yet as Dean falls in love with Ray, he forgets the shameful origins of their courtship. When Ray and Dean arrive together at the "homeplace"—the very land Percy aims to steal—"part of [Dean] genuinely want[s] to warn Ray, to protect him" (Kenan, 1992, p. 176). But as Ray invites him into the house, Dean immerses himself in this space teeming with Ray's experience and memory, palpable with the life of the man he deeply desires. Dean's ethical sense eludes him as he moves into a sensual relationship with Ray:

> Dean, naked, stood with his back to Ray, those tender fingers exploring the joints and the hinges of his body; as a wet, warm tongue outlined, ever so lightly, the shape of his gooseflesh-cold body, Ray mumbling trance-like (All flesh is grass, my love, sweet, sweet grass) between bites, between pinches; as they slid into the plump feather bed that *scree-eee-creeked* as they lay there, underneath a quilt made by Ray's great-grandmother, multicolored, heavy; as they joined at the mouth. (Kenan, 1992, p. 176)

Through this voluptuous description, Kenan discloses an erotic truth repressed in the white male conception of Southern place. If Percy's attachment to the land represents marred relationships to self and other—relationships the conventional white male subject refuses to acknowledge and explore—Dean's relationship to Ray in this scene represents a deepened intimacy and communication between men, white and black. The sensuality between men and the communication across races suggest a reversal in the process by which the dominant conception of Southern place is formed. In fact, the natural imagery intermingled with the body ("all flesh is grass") suggests the undoing of the racist boundaries that, according to white superiority and demand, cordon off the landscape and its ownership. Though the dominant conception of Southern place rests on what white masculinity disavows, Kenan reveals a Southern place where desire and history are returned to consciousness.

Kenan thus provides a glimpse of the white male subject's recovery of a complex "libidinal language" (Silverman, 2000). The story, however, rests on the tragedy behind this recovery. That is, Dean discovers an intimacy between white and black men through a betrayal of the black man he loves. The sensual bond that Kenan (1992) depicts, therefore, opens onto the historical implications of Dean's betrayal:

> As Dean trembled and tingled and clutched—all the while in his ears he heard a noise: faint at first, then loud, louder, then deafening: and he was not sure if the quickening *thu-thump-thump, thu-thump-thump* of his heartbeat came from Ray's bites on his nipples

> or from fear. Dean felt certain he heard the voices of old black men and old black women screaming for his death, his blood, for him to be strung up on a Judas tree, to die and breathe no more. (pp. 176–177)

Just as history intrudes on Dean's conscience, Percy bursts into Ray's bedroom with dogs and a Polaroid camera. This Southern "homeplace" thus becomes a site of sensuality *and* violence, intimacy *and* trauma. Moreover, as a dissection of the white male attachment to Southern place, it exposes that attachment as a betrayal of one's own desire. Kenan moves from the trauma of history, from the ghosts of the past Dean has heard, to the personal loss Dean now suffers, revealing their inextricable entanglement:

> Dean began to shiver; more than anything else he could imagine at that moment, he wanted Ray to hold him. . . . He reached out and saw his pale hand against the broad bronze back and sensed the enormity of what he had done, that his hand could never again touch that back, never glide over its ridges and bends and curves, never linger over that mole, pause at this patch of hair, that scar. (p. 182)

Dean's guilt is an obvious symbol of the universal guilt that haunts white Southerners, a guilt that is, nonetheless, continually disavowed while being acted out. We see it acted out as "Run, Mourner, Run" unfolds. Percy successfully blackmails Ray and steals his land. Shunned by Percy, Dean loses Ray and his job. And the image of Dean sitting in the swing, embedded in the landscape, returns, resonating with all of these losses, even referencing the lynching noose. Dean mournfully scrapes at the land for meaning but refuses to grasp his complicity in Percy's racism and deviousness: "Dean Williams gazes down now at the trough in the earth in which his feet have been sliding. For eighteen years. Sliding. The red clay hard and baked after years of sun and rain and little-boy feet. Exposed" (Kenan, 1992, p. 172).

Having lost Ray, Dean hazards collecting the money Percy promised him. Percy and his sons violently refuse Dean's demand. Dean thus remains alienated from both the black man he loves and the white man with whom he tragically identified. In his alienation, we see the deep subjective consequences of the white male refusal to acknowledge the complex foundations of Southern place:

> He sat in some strange limbo, some odd place of ghosts and shadows, knowing he must rise . . . knowing he would be late for supper, knowing he could never really explain, never really tell anyone what had happened, knowing he would surely die one day, hoping it would be now. He could not move. (Kenan, 1992, p. 188)

The character of Dean Williams recalls characters from William Faulkner's fiction. In the characters of Ike McCaslin and Quentin Compson, Faulkner represents the Southern white man's tragic inability to work through his relationship to past and place. In "Run, Mourner, Run," Kenan returns to the problem of this melancholic stasis. Moreover, he explores this form of subjectivity in a way that unsettles its relationship to Southern place. Susan Donaldson (1999) argues that in our return to Faulkner's characters, literary figures that represent a binding ambivalence toward Southern place, we "risk echoing past concerns and past monologues—those defined by fear of change and difference" (p. 665). We risk, in other words, further grounding "narrow and exclusionary definitions of Southern identity and Southern literature" (p. 664). Against this tendency, Kenan emphasizes the complex fabric of desires and identifications that underlie the Faulknerian white male subject and, therefore, disallows the treatment of this figure as the tragic hero and defining character of Southern place.

Quentin and Ike long for the purity of a place in history. Their tragic fates—suicide and a repudiation of the land (which I read as a repudiation of life in the world)—represent their inability to understand identity in terms other than unity and authority. Kenan's presentation of this predicament, I believe, emphasizes the impossibility and tragic social and subjective consequences of the aspiration to white male purity. Kenan shows that identification with hegemonic white masculinity negates interracial intimacy, identification, and empathy, and that it diminishes the capacity to grasp one's life in terms of history and the complexities of place.

Kenan refigures the traditional meaning of the Southern land. Through the character of Dean Williams, he represents a disruption, although an ultimately tragic one, in the alignment of white male subjectivity and Southern place. He thus undermines the imaginary link between Southern place and coherent community.

In the next section, I turn to the work of another African American writer who examines the complexity of Southern place. Like Randall Kenan, Reginald McKnight rereads race and gender bonds embedded in perceptions of place. Whereas Kenan works through the traditional trope of the land, McKnight exposes the South that coheres around the experience of placelessness, an experience the Nashville Agrarians marked as a threat to the Southern way of life.

The Race and Gender of Placelessness: Reginald McKnight's "The White Boys"

I am drawn to Reginald McKnight's (1998) novella "The White Boys" out of an autobiographical impulse. The title challenges my sense of identity. The novella's setting—Louisiana in the late 1960s—invites me to search within the narrative for my experience of home. And the story's deeply subjective representation of place compels my interest in the role of place in self-formation.

Though I am drawn to "The White Boys" out of an impulse toward the familiar, the story has become embedded in my experience and research because of its unsettling effects. The story disrupts my expectations about what I might find in an autobiographically resonant tale of identity, home, and place. Mary Aswell Doll (2000) values the use of fiction in curriculum theorizing because it introduces unfamiliar worlds. "The White Boys" inspires my thoughts about curriculum because it raises my sense of the familiar but provides, as Doll writes, a "shock of confrontation with that which is utterly Other" (p. xv).

Three features of McKnight's novella unsettle my secure "sense of place" in narrative. First, "The White Boys" examines *white* male identity through a *black* male character's subjection to *white* male fantasies. It thus exposes the oppressive consequences of the white male effort to achieve the cultural ideal of white masculinity. Second, the novella introduces the problem of Southern place through the theme of placelessness. While for Donald Davidson and the Nashville Agrarians, the absence of a "sense of place" was the greatest threat to identity and culture, one projected onto the North and the Northern-influenced academy, McKnight reminds us that displacement and painful wandering are fundamental to a region steeped in racial antagonism and historical forgetting. The third aspect of this narrative that disrupts my taken-for-granted view of the world is its depiction of a racialized emotional inheritance in white men. More specifically, the novella shows how parental identifications can support racism in white male subjectivity. In what follows, I examine these three aspects of the narrative: racist fantasy, placelessness, and a white male emotional inheritance.

In the "The White Boys" McKnight explores subtle movements of racial antipathy in the Deep South, specifically within and between two families—one black, one white—whose dissonant encounters with each other reverberate in the characters' individual fantasies and memories. The two families, the Oates and the Hookers, live next door to each other in Louisiana, and their proximity and the conflicts between them evoke a larger field of racial tensions rooted in Southern history. In the opening pages, the South's history of racial violence is made "present, relevant, even urgent" (p. 117) for the main character, Derrick Oates, when his friend warns him about the dangers for blacks living in the Deep South. The friend's brief but explicit description of a lynching scene leaves Derrick in thrall to a history that he cannot grasp and therefore has few ways of working through. McKnight maps the seepage of this history through subjective and interpersonal terrain, showing the disturbance of racist meanings within everyday experiences and identifications. As Derrick's struggle to comprehend this unfathomable past unsettles his family and neighbors, it illuminates the problem of confronting the legacy of racism in the South. No American, Northerner or Southerner, easily confronts racism. McKnight's narrative, however, suggests something particular about that struggle in the South. When Southern place serves as a panacea for subjective and social alienation, it conceals the effects of racism and diminishes our capacity to transform race relations.

Set in the late 1960s, "The White Boys" speaks to that historical moment in the American South when the public ideology of white supremacy was met with resistance, activating a civil rights movement. More specifically, the narrative reveals the racism that persisted through that era even as public discourses began to veil white dominance. As I've argued, the discourse of Southern place itself has had this concealing effect.

McKnight situates the narrative historically by laying bare racial conflicts associated with the civil rights movement. We follow Derrick Oates in his experience of integration in the South. Derrick is one of the few black students in his school. Though he feels he has become accustomed to this, his teacher magnifies his experience of difference by suggesting he would be more comfortable in the all-black school across town. Derrick's classmates alienate him with hostile pranks. And his white neighbors draw him into a violent racist fantasy when they feel Derrick has encroached upon their homeplace.

Through the story, we see how Derrick's family negotiates difficult contact with their white neighbors. Despite better intentions, Southerners persist in their racism, even against the grain of the civil rights challenge. Derrick's mother, Portia Oates, for example, listens to her neighbor nervously dismiss the significance of a "whites only" sign on a local business—the white woman "act[ing] as though she could explain it all away" (McKnight, 1998, pp. 186–187). After she experiences this woman's attempt to consign racism to the past, Portia begins to perceive the Southern landscape differently. She thinks that the South has begun to "look like every place in this country she had ever been" (p. 187). In the face of her neighbors' attempt to submerge a virulent racism in polite language, Portia reflects on her disorientation about Southern place, and the idea of social standing merges with physical placement: "I know and I don't know where I am" (p. 188).

Finally, McKnight (1998) roots his story in the civil rights historical moment by uncovering more explicit white racist responses to interracial intimacy. The Oates' neighbor Eugene Hooker represents those who most fear the heightened intimacy of black and white; blacks, he believes, are "drawn to us like moths to light" (p. 172). The sexual nature of Eugene's fear is revealed as his thoughts turn to miscegenation: "They want their boys to sneak up, mix in, lighten up the herd a bit" (p. 172). As Eugene warns his wife and sons about the black neighbors who have moved in next door, McKnight more fully exposes the racism that persists despite the civil rights movement's public challenge to white supremacy. Eugene says:

> [A] lot has changed in this country in the years we were gone. Colored people, lately, as you can see on the TV and the papers, have been getting louder and more dangerous every day. . . . They're killing white people by the hundreds, turning our kids on to drugs, and pimping our girls. (p. 149)

While place becomes integrated, psychic space remains prejudicial, fearful of *and* fascinated with an encroaching other.

The Terrain of Fantasy

While situating us historically, McKnight also moves below the conscious symbolic textures of Southern place to situate us in a terrain of fantasy. More specifically, he shows how the region harbors the white fantasy of absolute racial difference and how that fantasy infects relationships to self and others.

McKnight points to the terrain of fantasy at the foundation of Southern place by presenting characters that are not consciously identified with Southern place but deeply entangled with its racist history and politics. These characters are not conspicuously Southern. As we recall from the story, the father of each of the two families is an air force sergeant who, after a tour of duty during the Vietnam War, has moved to the South to continue his military service. The South does not provide these characters solace, nor does it ground their senses of identity. Southern history and place nonetheless bind their lives.

The "fantasmatic" (Silverman, 1992, pp. 3–10) quality of the South thus emerges in the tension between the story's theme of Southern place and the characters' senses of dislocation, as evidenced by Portia's vertigo, which strikes into the very heart of her being and yet brings her to stasis: "I know and I don't know where I am" (p. 188). The characters are preoccupied with the South. But the Southern landscape provides no ground for them; it only exacerbates their fixations on regional movements and differences. We see—through McKnight's colloquial rendering of thought and memory—that a sense of rootlessness pervades the minds of the characters. Portia, for example, contemplates how "prejudice manifest[s] itself as variously as vegetation from region to region," and ultimately acknowledges that "new places [are] just enough different to make her feel unsure of everything, even the familiar" (McKnight, 1998, p. 188). For her son Derrick, on the other hand, new places still have promise. He imagines that "every place [brings] out something new in the world, and in you" (p. 116). And yet, being the character most attuned to place, Derrick witnesses, during his first days in Louisiana, the South's persistent underlying threat of violence. McKnight writes: "Louisiana rain, Derrick thought, falls like lead, like it's shot from a gun" (p. 116). In this way, he reveals how ungrounded and, indeed, vulnerable Derrick feels in a region mythologized for the deep sense of place it supposedly affords its inhabitants. As in the novels of Walker Percy, a sense of estrangement and vacancy imbues this South. While Percy's Southerners defend against history by wandering through an unreal present, however, McKnight's characters are without guard against the sting of a repressed historical past.

The Dynamics of Racist Fantasy

In many ways, "The White Boys" stages the realm of racist fantasy that underlies the dominant discourse of Southern place.[15] Before more specifically exemplifying this aspect of the narrative, I want to characterize the dynamics of fantasy. To do so, I turn again to Lacanian psychoanalytic theory.

Lacan explains that fantasy is "an image set to work in a signifying structure" (quoted in Evans, 1996, p. 61). In other words, through a visual image, fantasy introduces that which is beyond language, the disturbance of the Real into our process of meaning-making. Following Lacan, Slavoj Žižek (1998) argues that fantasy is the ideological support for a particular version of reality. He disputes the idea that fantasy simply veils the features of a reality we can grasp. In other words, he insists we cannot break through fantasy to arrive in a state of the really real. The belief that we can fully grasp reality represents an attachment to the idea of subjective unity and totality, which refers back to Lacan's famous articulation of the mirror stage. On the contrary, Žižek argues, fantasy is a fundamental function of subjectivity that buffers against the Real as it also expresses an irreducible lack in being. It is a measure of consistency in the face of subjective contingency and antagonism. Fantasy supports our dwelling within language and is always bound up with ideology. Ideological fantasy, therefore, grounds our sense of reality, our belief systems and prejudices, and our conscious identifications and beliefs.

Fantasy also structures self/other relationships. It embodies scenarios that give shape to desire and position us in relation to objects and other people. The subjective lack that fantasy contains, or for which it compensates, therefore, is projected onto objects and others in the social field. If fantasy structures our desire for others, it also marks others as excessive and threatening, as something "too massive, [and] too close" (Žižek, 1998, p. 167). Fantasies, then, are not merely intrapsychically held. Indeed, insofar as versions of reality are imposed on particular communities and collectivities, containing the threat and excess in the Other, fantasies structure the social field. This aberrance in fantasy, imposed on others, causes hatred and intolerance wherever a lack is perceived.

Žižek (1998) also refers specifically to a "racist fantasmatic"—a system of fantasies structured by the belief in an absolute "duality of blacks and whites" (p. 67). He argues white racist fantasy aligns blackness with lack, marking it as a threatening and excessive force. Lack therefore begins as something internal, but is projected onto the external other, which in turn, becomes hostile and threatening. With this, we can return to the way McKnight situates us in the system of fantasies that dominate the South.[16] In "The White Boys" Derrick Oates confronts—has the capacity to see, or at least to glimpse—the white fantasy structuring the social field in which he is caught, the racist fantasy that binds him to "the white boys" who are his neighbors and who, in fact, turn him against himself. Coinciding with Lacan's description of the fantasy as a frozen scene (Evans, 1996, p. 60), what Derrick confronts is a lynching tableau.

The Violence of the Landscape

Derrick's recollections map out the Oates' journey over the years, from California through Colorado and Texas to Louisiana, a gradual journey into the Deep South. While remembering this movement, Derrick reflects on his experience of racism in each of the places he has lived. In Louisiana, his family stands out for having chosen to live near the air force base instead of in the black neighborhood across town.

McKnight first evokes the fantasy terrain of the South by situating the main character in a visual experience that is beyond the reach of language. The narrative opens with Derrick Oates looking through a window as rain and wind pound the Louisiana landscape. In this scene, Derrick sees that, unlike the rain of his previous homes, this rain "breaks things to pieces, makes birds disappear, eats everything up" (McKnight, 1998, pp. 115–116). Derrick witnesses something excessive in the rainstorm, a destructive yet animating force. When "the lightning flashe[s] with the constancy of a strobe," he sees "the world . . . go white" and hears thunder sound "from behind miles of cloud" (p. 116)

As Derrick looks at the landscape, McKnight points to experience that remains outside consciousness and the reach of language. He states specifically that the startling rain moves Derrick "unconsciously" as he sees the world "go white" (McKnight, 1998, p. 116), suggesting a frame for the fantasy that will make Derrick both an insider and an outsider at once. McKnight then marks the latency of Derrick's speech and thought: "If he had been able to, Derrick would have said that every place brought out something new in the world" (p. 116). Again indicating the limits of Derrick's language in terms of place, McKnight writes: "[T]here was always something about a new place that excited him in ways he couldn't put into words" (p. 116). Where language fails, the fantasy realm of Southern place emerges.

In this scene, Derrick remembers places and experiences that have led him here, to his life in Louisiana. Remembering the past, Derrick confronts a rupture in the natural surroundings of the Louisiana landscape, an embodiment of the historical violence widespread in the Deep South. The rain, McKnight writes, "battered," "guillotined," "pummeled," and "plastered" the landscape of Derrick's new home (McKnight, 1998, p. 115). The landscape also adumbrates fragments of a lynching scene, a scene that will beleaguer Derrick throughout the story. From the window of his living room, Derrick witnesses an uncanny intermingling of history and place. As he recalls it, "*Ropes* of dark green water rushed the leaves down gutters. The green water *twisted* down drains. . . . Steam *hung* low to the ground, and overhead, lighting *flared* through clouds thick as moon dust" (my emphasis, p. 115). In the landscape, Derrick sees ropes, twisted, hung, flared.

This depiction of the setting resonates, though subtly, with the violence of lynching, a form of violence Derrick has previously learned about from a friend.

Derrick recalls this conversation as he looks out at the rain. While living in Texas, Derrick has heard as a warning from his friend John Powers that in the Deep South "they lynch coloreds down there for nothing." "I can't believe you guys didn't know that," John says. "They tie 'em up, cut off their balls, burn 'em, maybe eat 'em too" (McKnight, 1998, p. 118). This lynching tableau, mobilized through John's bravado, violently invades Derrick. Derrick tries, on hearing about this violence, to first dispute it among his friends and then to strike it from his thoughts. The lynching scene, however, inevitably takes hold of him:

> The barbecue smell on the night air sickened him, and he felt a cold tremor in his chest. He wouldn't let himself think the words, That's what it must smell like. He wouldn't let himself see images of people cooking penises on the grill. He wouldn't imagine charred flesh, or screams, or the nasty laughter of white men. He squeezed his crossed arms tighter together, and held back the shiver, which dissipated everywhere through his body, but would not enter his head, his mind. (p. 119)

Derrick's subjection to the lynching image disturbingly provides the narrative continuity in an otherwise circuitous and digressive story. The image functions like a secret, compelling Derrick's search for understanding, functioning on the underside of his relationship with others. Contesting the Agrarian tradition, McKnight seems to suggest that this violent fragment of history is concealed within a pastoral vision of Southern place but will not stay dormant or hidden. It signals the return of the repressed. After the violent image seizes Derrick's mind, the narrative again focuses on the rain. "The rain slackened for a moment," McKnight writes. "Then suddenly the rain dropped by the bucketful and the wind exploded with a momentary gust that bent every tree and bush" (p. 119).

What stands out here is the way McKnight embeds the lynching scene and Derrick's subjection to it within both memory and nature. For the black man, the landscape as place is not a comforting seat of identity, not a means of reifying a fantasy of belonging born out of lack, but a derisive and truly threatening reminder of the violent history upon which white supremacy is founded. Derrick recalls it—half consciously—as he looks out at the rain wreaking havoc on his new Louisiana home. This introduction to the narrative, therefore, provides an image of the deep roots of racist violence in Southern psychology, history, and place. All of this occurs within the first few pages of a story written in "a prose that is at times exceedingly plain" (Cooper, 1998) and that foregrounds everyday interracial contact rather than the extreme act of violence that initiates the narrative. McKnight therefore situates us in the layers of history and fantasy that are interwoven into the everyday textures of Southern place.

The narrative follows Derrick in his struggle to understand identity as a location, as one's shifting position in family, school, and society. As Derrick grapples with the vicissitudes of his place in the world, we see the historical trauma of racial violence infuse his everyday experiences and the experiences of those around him. This history travels through secrets, it haunts gestures, and it invades the characters' mere glimpses of their ambient world. A trace of history wreaks havoc on memory and relationships. Derrick's mother witnesses racism in the landscape, growing "everywhere, abundant, dense, floral, prickly; [growing] in broad, flat jungle leaves, and in lichen scabs upon stones" (McKnight, 1998, p. 188). Derrick's father understands that it lies "beneath the skin like an insect larva in a chrysalis" (p. 198). Indeed, it is ingrained within the very veins of the landscape. Derricks feels it in a gaze, "prickling the back of his neck, grazing his left cheek, burning the collar of his shirt like a beam of light through a magnifying glass" (p. 170). These metaphors and similes suggest that racism is interwoven with our surroundings, embedded in place, as a tacit yet binding force. And for the black man, the master narrative is a fossil print within any spectral view he takes of the landscape. It is already determined as a place in which he does not belong, a place where his own lack is never nullified. McKnight thus calls the reader to recognize how racist history infects our world, at times as a strangely nebulous presence.

The White Boys

McKnight exposes racial antagonism working at the level of the unconscious. He dramatically represents the way a violent racist image, a trace of history, becomes infused in Derrick's unconscious experience. McKnight does not suggest, however, that this history is intrapsychically bound. "White boys" have imposed the lynching image on Derrick and, as Derrick attempts to make sense of it, the image seizes the attention of "the white boys" around him. The unconscious that McKnight reveals, therefore, is a cultural unconscious, a "transindividual dynamic" living between individuals and within social formations, a dynamic that, as Dean (2000) argues, is interwoven with our perceptions of landscape and place (p. 2).

Alongside Derrick's growing awareness of the politics of place and identity, the story provides a close-up of the development of racism in the thoughts and behaviors of two "white boys": Garret Hooker and his father, Eugene. On his first day of school, Derrick had gradually become aware that Garret has him fixed in his gaze. "Slowly, degree by degree," McKnight (1998) writes, "Derrick began to notice that the stocky redhead sitting one row over and one seat behind him was staring at him with the intensity of a heat lamp" (p. 169). He is thus scorched by the redheaded boy, whose gaze, it seems, can penetrate the color of Derrick's skin, to get to the core of its meaning. At the end of the school day, Derrick discovers that this white boy is his neighbor.

The narrative creates tension in the relationship between the young boys but then digresses to expose Eugene Hooker's racism, thus emphasizing the familial pathways racism travels. On seeing the Oates family move in next door, Eugene becomes focused on their behavior, his racial hatred surfacing from a taciturn and "dour" demeanor. Although Eugene is a racist, he recalls a loving friendship he had with a black friend, Dennis, when he was a young boy. He recalls as well feeling betrayed when Dennis began to identify more deeply with black culture and history. Eugene expresses disgust as he remembers Dennis's talk of "our heritage," of "Pan-Africa and Mali, and pyramids and shit" (McKnight, 1998, p. 178). A loss of intimacy with a black friend has shaken Eugene's white world. This loss resonates with his sense of being abandoned by his mother. Moving toward the deeper source of his racial confusion, Eugene recalls the way his mother related with the black people in their neighborhood, that she was "drawn to them, easy with them, talked like them, after a while, like it was her first language" (McKnight, 1998, p. 172). Eugene believes blacks have tainted his relationship to a secure maternal world. McKnight finally arrives at the source of Eugene's racism as he explains that "when Hooker's mother married [a] black man, he sealed his heart beneath miles of cold wax, and stone and water, and stopped believing in anything that began or ended with black people" (p. 178).

With Eugene's personal history laid bare, McKnight returns to the relationship between the two boys. That relationship, we discover, has developed into a friendship. It nonetheless bears the violent history that has burdened Derrick throughout the narrative. Disturbed by his thoughts of lynching, Derrick has searched for and found evidence of lynching in a history book. As Derrick's new friend, Garret has begun to share in the confusion about the lynching images. McKnight, therefore, represents the history of racial violence as an uncanny interracial bond, not unlike Kenan's construction of an uncanny interracial bond between Ray and Dean in "Run, Mourner, Run."

When Eugene discovers the relationship between the two boys, his repressed past threatens to return. Rather than confront the past, Eugene plans to frighten the boys away from each other, furthering the repression that so beleaguers him. McKnight makes the violence of such repression clear as Eugene asks his son to punish Derrick for violating racial boundaries. "Are you ready to do something very strong to teach him a lesson?" Eugene asks. "Are you gonna be a man with me on this?" (p. 179). Like Kenan, McKnight depicts the white male subject caught in conflicting identifications, caught between interracial intimacy and violent white male authority. He thus further illuminates the white male anxiety of insufficiency at the foundation of Southern place.

A Racialized Inheritance and the Gendering of Place

At the end of McKnight's story, the character Garret Hooker (the redheaded boy) becomes ill because he harbors emotions that he does not fully own. The friendship he extends to his black schoolmate Derrick teems with hatred. Feeling acutely both an affinity with Derrick and the racial enmity his father and the South have bequeathed to him, Garret represents white male subjectivity in the throes of a racialized emotional inheritance. The double bind Garret faces and the psychological turmoil he and his father share illuminate the disturbance of otherness at the foundation of the hegemonic white male subject. Through stream-of-consciousness narration, we learn that Hooker feels the presence of black people "like [a] shadow, always there, even in the dark" (McKnight, 1998, p. 172). Mapping the complexity of this feeling, McKnight reveals how this shadowy disturbance must be understood not only as a source of hatred but also as the effect of a repressed longing for the racial other. Eugene Hooker, we see, uses black men to "focus his hate" and "focus his pity, which he put[s] in the place of love" (pp. 177–178). Uncovering the emotional complexity of racist subjectivity, McKnight reminds us that racial prejudice is a psychical process rather than a monolithic subjective state, that the emotional registers or "structures of feeling" (Williams, 1977. p. 32) that support racist society are not reducible to outright hatred. Moreover, he reminds us that those structures of feeling are held between people and within parental identifications. When Eugene's racist "mood and words, his nervousness" make his son Garret "sick with anxiety" (McKnight, 1998, p. 154), it becomes clearer that the social field is marred by a white male inheritance—a white male disavowal of interracial history, culture, and intimacy.

As Garret suffers his father's "moods and words," he relies on his mother to provide solace. McKnight therefore reveals the way the mother serves as a protective harbor for beleaguered white masculinity. When Eugene's racism explodes in front of his family, Garret escapes to his room with "his mind . . . hot from the things his father had said" (McKnight, 1998, p. 154). In his room, Garret waits for his mother to rescue him from the racist demands his father has placed on him: "Garret's brow grew fevered from these thoughts, and he was never happier to see his mother as she stepped into his room [that] night" (p. 154). Tonya enters to soothe the anguish Garret's father has imposed on him, ushering in the perspective of a woman on Southern place and its racial dimensions. "She wore her long nightgown," Garret recalls, "the one with the pink roses all over it, and Dad's old blue robe, which she wore more often than he did" (p. 154). Tonya's appearance and behavior suggest how she tends to the threadbare emotions of her husband and family:

> Long ravels hung all over [her] robe, and it was completely worn through at the elbows. She pulled at the ravels as she spoke, but she never broke them off. . . . And her voice seemed the same way, too, a gentle pulling sound . . . that drew every tension from his mind and body, leaving him slack and grateful. (pp. 154–155)

As she comforts her son, Tonya moves toward condemning her husband's racism. But she ultimately fails to do so. Instead, she explains away his racism in romanticized pastoral language about the diversity of human experience. In her speech, Eugene's racial hatred is reduced to one of the many things in the ground that nourishes "the flowers in [her] garden" (p. 155). Her speech recalls the pastoral language that supports white masculinity in the South, thus exposing the alignment of that discourse with the mother. In this private familial scene, McKnight reveals the gendering of place that persistently conceals the region's history of trauma, beginning with the site of severance. Tonya explains to her son that people, like the flowers in her garden, can't "very well grow in soil without water, or water without soil. They need all sorts of things to grow, like sunshine, soil, rain, even wind" (p. 155).

The comfort Tonya Hooker provides to her son illuminates the gendering of Southern place. The Southern white men in this story lack a "sense of place" to palliate the disturbance of racial antagonism in their lives. Their wives and mothers serve as moorings in the face of this placelessness. McKnight thus shows how men use women to "have a room of their own," how "the woman's space turns into absorption in the mother" and how the mother then "ceases to exist" (Frosh, 1994, p. 130). McKnight then exposes the white male "dwelling in the woman" compelled by the dominant conception of Southern place (p. 130).

Conclusion

These two narratives explored in this chapter unsettle the Agrarian image of the white male subject in his relationship to land and landscape. The short story "Run, Mourner, Run" emphasizes the land as the fundamental figure of Southern place. Refiguring the land, the story significantly challenges the autochthonous ideal, disrupting this emergence trope of white male Southern identity. It ultimately reveals the land to be a conduit of complex social relationships and subjective experiences. "The White Boys," on the other hand, depicts a Southern place that is losing its concrete moorings, becoming placeless, but that remains enthralling to its inhabitants. This story exposes a vertiginous rather than comforting Southern "sense of place," a sense of place bound up with racial antagonism. In the absence of the traditional, grounding "sense of place," the story traces this racial antagonism through familial relations, paternal and maternal identifications, and interracial intimacies. Together these narratives invite me to interrogate my own relationship to the American South, to explore the autobiographical roots of my knowledge about the region and to develop a more capacious understanding of my place in it.

AUTOBIOGRAPHICAL INTERLUDE

Opening the Landscape to Questions of Identity and History

[W]e cannot consciously choose the visual "words" through which our past will be respoken. . . . All that we can do is answer the appeal which comes to us from the world to find our memories in its forms.

—Kaja Silverman (2000, p. 145)

The elements of place to which we are most responsive (consciously or unconsciously) comprise the physical signs of our deepest intentions and desires.

—Gerald Kennedy (1990, p. 500)

Otherness and familiarity are reinforced by impressions of landscape.

—Lucy Lippard (1997, p. 61)

The rain holds my thoughts. Throughout May and June, rainstorms have soaked the South Louisiana landscape. These are the rains of my youth, intense downpours that seem to distend the envelope of space I imagine to be my home. This rain moves in like a memory, arriving before I'm ready, washing out a sinkhole where an oak tree once stood, carrying last year's fallen leaves to my doorstep. If landscapes confront us with absence and distance,[17] this rain returns, however indistinctly, what the landscape has lost. The rain gives an unmistakable presence to place, making place seem overfull, excessive, teeming with something long deferred. Pushing at the boundaries of home, marking the impermanence of that very phenomenon, the rain reveals to me the deeply subjective character of place and the way place influences the creation of self.

When I was a young boy, the rains would flood the banks of the Amite River, seep into a neighboring creek, and gradually fill, to heights of five feet, the suburban landscape in which I rode my bicycle and played baseball with my friends. When the water rose, our houses remained just out of its reach, as the remnant woods and fields linking our suburban homes became swampland. We then navigated our backyards in pirogues and bateaus until the blazing summer sun returned us to dry land. Time and again, we saw the landscape transformed and then restored to familiar conditions. In this way, Louisiana rainstorms taught me about the mutability and persistence of place, about the experience of losing and rediscovering some fundamental ground for being-in-the-world.

The rain also evokes memories of self-shattering fear. When the rains rapped with heavy hands on our doors and windows and the winds wailed against our home, I saw my mother in the throes of emotion I believed to be alien to her character. The rains submerged my mother in dread. They undid her confidence and authority and therefore seemed able to soak through to some elemental flaw in our family, capable of washing our family away. I remember my family clustered together in our car, racing in front of a violent storm on the way to visit my mother's parents in Natchitoches, Louisiana; the storm descending on us as we arrived; and my mother forgetting us—our becoming lost to her—as she found a nook in her parents' bedroom to embrace her collapse. At our home in Baton Rouge, when a storm raged, she asked us to lie on the floor in the hallway as she covered us with blankets, this her last gesture of motherly protection before her retreat, her slippage from control. Tapping my mother's deepest fears, the rains introduced me to the vulnerability in family and home, the vulnerability in my protective surroundings.

My mother's intense fear of the rain and wind marks my memory. In a way, her fear became my own. More importantly perhaps, it has recently become a source of conversation between us about the demands of gender roles in our lives. Upon reading my above recollections, my mother began to speak about the experiences of motherhood that are connected to her fear of the rain. She explained that idealizations of motherhood leave little room for the fear, ambivalence, and sense of loss that mothering inevitably entails. She recalled a conversation in which we discussed Adrienne Rich's (1976/1986) *Of Woman Born*, specifically Rich's account of "the suffering of ambivalence" that infuses her care for her children (pp. 21–22). "Mothers must find ways to express and understand these emotions that run counter to the roles and expectations that have been placed on them," my mother explains. "The rain for me must have been a continual reminder of that need, inviting emotions that motherhood caused me to ignore" (J. Casemore, personal communication, June 20, 2006).

My mother describes the need to make space within her life for experience that her role as Mother seemed to exclude. Similarly, as Rich discusses her early days of motherhood, she recounts experiencing the home as a hermetic realm or "magnetic field" where "the enormity and inevitability" of the love she felt for her child, which she believed was required of her, forestalled "any attempt to salvage [herself]" (pp. 22–23). Rich also relates the power of the natural metaphor to obscure the life of the mother: "[T]he emotion-charged, tradition-heavy form in which I found myself cast as the Mother seemed . . . as ineluctable as the tides" (pp. 23–24). Upon reading these lines, my mother began to share stories about her own struggle to make space for herself within motherhood, a struggle that has, she points out, been veiled by her fear of the rain.

My mother's explanation of her fear of the rain helps me make sense of my own. I recall being afraid of the rain in my childhood, but I remember as well being drawn toward the chaos and threat. I remember seeking in a rainstorm the experience of being overwhelmed. A character in Don DeLillo's (1982) novel *The Names* speaks of "a period of curious fear between the first sweet-smelling breeze and the time when the rain comes cracking down" (p. 303). For me, that unsettling duration was a threshold for the imagination, a breach in reality in which I could lose myself. Being so moved by the threat of rain, I felt this curious fear evolve into my sense of being inspired by the world around me. The risk and promise of coming undone in a storm enlivened my desire to linger at the boundary of the knowable. I remember riding my bicycle around our neighborhood block as a hurricane approached. My mother had called us in. The streets, usually teeming with children, were uncannily empty. The whirling wind collected dust and leaves around me—at one moment aiding my movement, and at another forcing me into the curb or coaxing me to a standstill. I remember then finding a path between severe gusts and moving along as if the wind and I had a shared purpose. And I remember my defiance when my mother called for me again, my desire to continue riding beyond her voice, and my need to tuck myself into the imminence of the storm.

The rain is a crucial symbol in my experience of home and place. It taps into deep senses of attachment and separation. It introduces my identification with my mother and my experience of the maternal. And it calls forth a personal narrative that demonstrates the embedding of the social world in subjective experience. I now want to further address the relationships this narrative adumbrates, yet at a different level of autobiographical inquiry.

Exploring the psychical reverberations of a personal trope (such as the rain) or a cathected environment (such as a rural landscape) can create a sketch of subjective and social relationships that influence our lives. Working within a psychoanalytic framework, I value this level of self-narration because it discloses the workings of the unconscious. And it represents, however partially or guardedly, the fabric of attachments and detachments, identifications and disidentifications that contribute to a sense of self. However, to remain within the emotional valence of such narratives precludes the critical distance necessary for gaining insight into the relationships they disclose. Without that critical distance, rather than prefiguring insight, the narratives remain symbols of "authoritative selfhood" (Bersani, 1990, p. 3).

I want to open the above narrative to "experiential theorizing," an approach that acknowledges and unsettles the imaginary unity of the self, while also revealing the close relationship between theory and self-formation (Figlio & Richards, 2003, p. 407). Such theorizing fosters understanding of the unmarked conceptual and ideological ground of lived experience.

The rain conjures up the ambivalence in my experience of place, an ambivalence that extends to my comprehension of the South. When I drive from Baton Rouge to New Orleans, I pass into and out of numerous pockets of rain, meeting several times the threshold that marries storm and lighted sky. So many passages, so many capsules of rain and sun, remind me of the cultural complexity of Southern place, the heterogeneity of perspectives sustaining social and political tension in the American South. Like the most abiding of these rains, however, the designation "The South" has too often engulfed this complexity, reducing diverse histories to a sodden uniformity.

Moving through the rain between Baton Rouge and New Orleans, I think of the overall environmental conditions in this industrial corridor—where oil refineries and industrial plants flood millions of pounds of toxic waste into the air, water, and land each year, conditions that have earned the corridor the name Cancer Alley. Cancer Alley is home to many communities, most of them inhabited by poorer African Americans families. Though the communities have fought back with some success, recent research trends reveal an effort to further obscure the depth of this environmental racism (Goldfield, 2002, pp. 270–271; Koeppel, 1999).

As white Southerners continue to ignore the racism at the foundation of the region's cultural, educational, economic, and environmental struggles, it remains difficult to imagine regional identification—that is, Southernness—as something other than an effort to forget the region's racist history. The conception of society and its underside that Allen Tate presented in his 1938 novel *The Fathers* continues to bind Southern regional identity today: "Is not civilization the agreement, slowly arrived at, to let the abyss alone?" (quoted in Romine, 1999, p. 3).

Another Southern writer, the African American poet Yusef Komunyakaa, however, manages an ambivalent embrace of the South that suggests the possibility of not only confronting the abyss but also transforming the meaning of Southernness. Komunyakaa (2002b) describes the South as a "mecca of language and images" (p. 163). Having grown up in Bogalusa, Louisiana, a "hotbed for racism" in the 1950s and another site of environmental racism (Komunyakaa, 2002a, p. 98), he attempts to work through the internalization of the Southern landscape and "to refashion that inherited landscape through consciousness" (p. 163). His work reveals the real difficulty of that negotiation as Southern place continually threatens to become, like the hovering phosphorescent light he conjures up in the poem "Ignis Fatuus," "Nothing / but a presence that fills up / the mind, a replenished body / singing its way into doubletalk" (Komunyakkaa, 2003).

The rain imbues my private experiences of place, and it provides passageways into self-understanding. But it also draws me into larger histories. In Louisiana, intense rains inevitably conjure up tales of the way rainstorms have exacerbated the fierceness of another awe-inspiring feature of the region's landscape, the Mississippi River. Growing up, I often heard about the Great Flood of 1927. My great-grandmother specifically repeated a brief account of her narrow escape from the violent waters of the unchecked river. She spoke of her family's movement west from Avoyelles Parish as the rains fell and the river rose. She spoke of leaving with few belongings and traveling in a horse-drawn wagon. And she spoke of losing a home to the forces of nature.

In 1992 on my great-grandmother's hundredth birthday, nearly all one hundred and two of her descendants gathered with her to celebrate. Most of us still lived in or near the 1927 flood territory. After we found our names on the wall-sized family tree that connected us to Grandma Lemoine and to each other, the story of my grandmother's escape from the Great Flood was again the story we asked her to tell. My great-grandmother's memory infuses our own with a powerful belief, the belief that our lives and relationships can endure.

Though some stories of the Great Flood provide a sense of unity within family and community, there are other versions of the event to be told. From August 1926 until April 1927, rains devastated the central United States, relentlessly pounding several hundred thousand square miles of the Mississippi River valley. With the rains, the Mississippi River swelled. In the first months of 1927, ten separate flood crests moved down the river from Cairo, Illinois, to New Orleans. With the levees overburdened from Missouri and Illinois to the river's delta, the five worst rainstorms in ten years hit New Orleans. On April 15, the last of these storms dropped fifteen inches of rain in eighteen hours, leaving four feet of water standing in the streets. On that same day, severe rainstorms soaked the river valley area from Texas to Alabama and from Illinois to the Gulf of Mexico. On April 21, the levee broke at Mounds Landing, Mississippi. The water that flowed through that one crevasse covered an area fifty miles wide and one hundred miles long. The levees eventually gave way in numerous places along the river. All told, the Great Flood covered 27,000 square miles of land, lands inhabited by over 930,000 people (Barry, 1997).

In *Rising Tide*, John Barry (1997) unravels the historical context of the flood of 1927, documenting the deep interconnection between geophysical forces and social power. In Greenville, Mississippi—near the Mounds Landing crevasse—the battle against the flood intensified the racist politics of the region. As the rains fell and the river rose, thousands of black men were forced to labor on the weakening levees. Held at gunpoint and threatened with whips by white overseers, black men worked to fortify the levee—filling and hauling sandbags, building structures to impede erosion and raising the earth against the unrelenting river. When Greenville became inundated, the white power structure, fearing the permanent withdrawal of their agrarian labor force, refused to allow black men and women any means to evacuate. When the floodwaters subsided, black tenant farmers and farm owners were systematically denied aid from the Red Cross (pp. 378–395).

As secretary of commerce under Calvin Coolidge, Herbert Hoover headed the flood relief. With hopes for becoming the Republican candidate in the 1928 presidential election, Hoover quelled black protest against the injustices they experienced. Though the funding he generated was grossly inadequate and its distribution clearly racist, Hoover emerged as a hero and great humanitarian for his efforts to reconstruct the devastated flood region (Barry, 1997, pp. 378–395). Campaigning in part on his spurious achievements in the flood relief to Southern states, Hoover became the Republican candidate and won the 1928 presidential election in a landslide. As he secured vast numbers of white votes in the South, Hoover provided the foundation for a "competitive Republican Party in the South"—as Barry makes clear, "a 'lily white' Republican Party" (p. 413).

As the history of the Great Flood shows, Southern place is neither unified nor bound. Its meaning is irreducible to geography, history, literature, or subjectivity. It is a complex interweaving of these forces and the stories these forces exclude. Southern place informs, even binds, national politics (Pinar, 2004), speaks the region's history of racial violence, lives on in quotidian speech and memory, and continually transforms despite our efforts to fix and define it.

I have allowed the rain, a feature of the Southern landscape, to take me on a somewhat circuitous route through my experience and knowledge of place. Doing so, I collect disparate images and narratives of Southern place, creating tension—perhaps a "complicated conversation" (Pinar, 2004)—among them. I do so because I want to depict a process of self-formation that is inextricable from the geography, history, aesthetics, and politics of Southern place—inextricable, that is, from the dynamics that ensure Southern self-identification will remain fraught with complexity. What, more specifically, is the character of this educational undertaking?

The rain has shown me how the flow of thought meets the vicissitudes of place, making palpable the way internal reality is interwoven with particularities of the external world. The rain draws my eye to obscurities in the landscape of my home and inspires my reflection on the inclusions and exclusions of place. Place—my sense of place—is both substantiated and shattered by the rain. Writing about and working through (in the psychoanalytic sense) my experiences of the rain, therefore, promotes an intellectual confrontation with the ambivalences of place (McPherson, 2003, p. 216), a confrontation necessary for fostering "emotional registers," other than sentimentality and guilt, as "necessary and integral to southern identity" (p. 216). By stirring my memory and my connections to social history, the rain prompts social-psychoanalytic narration (Pinar, 2004), that is, "self-reflexive articulation of [my] subjectivity," where subjectivity is understood to be that "through which history and society speak" (p. 23). In my ongoing dialogue with place, the rain is a trope; it is a figure inscribed in the landscape, an expression that moves me—rhetorically—to inquire further into the language and history the landscape holds. What then is the nature of this language? How might we promote literacy in the language of landscape? How does one read and write to uncover the diverse histories of place?

In my penchant for the tumult of a storm, I also recognize the kernel of my curiosity about literature and art. Like the rains etched in my memory, the literary works I investigate in this book have complicated my sense of the worlds in which I live. They too have unveiled and taught me to value the tensions within my culturally diverse home; they have also at times left me mired in the opacity of the seemingly unbridgeable differences it contains. Literature and art have been for me consummate teachers about the self's conditions of change and stability—about the experience of ground, and the confrontation with the groundlessness of being. They have led me to ruptures in the fabric of my sense of the real. And they have proven to be the very stuff from which a life can be made when one is in the throes of such experiences of loss. Similar to the rainstorms of my youth, and the ones now cracking down on the world around me, art and literature offer places in which I might dwell, and unsettle the places where I have dwelled too long.

CHAPTER 4

Reshaping Our Inherited Landscape

Coming of age [in the South], I was fully aware of both the natural beauty and the social terror surrounding me.

—Yusef Komunyakaa (2002b, p. 163)

[P]lace is pedagogy demanding interrogation.

—Mary Aswell Doll (2000, p. 11)

Southern place demands interrogation because it holds a disturbing paradox, one occurring in the simultaneity of the South's capacity to fascinate and its perpetuation of social injustice. In the essay "Dark Waters" the African American poet Yusef Komunyakaa (2002a) addresses this very aspect of his hometown, Bogalusa, Louisiana, a place whose "beauty and horror," he explains, have "shaped the intensity of [his] observations" (p. 101). Appearing in *The Colors of Nature* (Deming & Savoy, 2002), a collection of essays that reads natural environments against the grain of Euro-American conceptions of place and wilderness, "Dark Waters" captures Komunyakaa's use of the landscape as an autobiographical, cultural, and historical text, and it demonstrates an understanding of place as a dynamic configuration of these forms of meaning.

Through the "smoke-dark waters" of the creek for which Bogalusa was named, Komunyakaa finds the ghosts and voices of the Native Americans who, deracinated and "suppressed to near extinction," continue to live "in a half glimpse, somewhere among the trees as elusive, nocturnal souls" (Komunyakaa, 2002a, pp. 98–100). Recalling both the "great towering pines" (p. 102) and the "saw vines and scrub oak" (p. 99) of his hometown, Komunyakaa moves through his memories of the Jim Crow South. He remembers not only the crosses that burned and Ku Klux Klan murders but also black resistance, resistance solidified in the Deacons for Defense and Justice, the Bogalusa-based group established to protect civil rights workers from the Klan. Finally, through the millpond near his childhood home—"always a place of ritual" (p. 101)—Komunyakaa begins to unravel the environmental racism suffered by African Americans in the Deep South. In doing so, he holds his readers in an inextricable weave of nature and culture, laying bare, like Kenan and McKnight, the lessons of place that we have been disinclined to learn.

"Perhaps we haven't learned nature's greatest instruction" (p. 102), Komunyakaa (2002a) patiently speculates. The consummate teacher, he then determinedly reminds us of the lesson we have ignored: "we are connected. Everything is connected" (p. 102). "Dark Waters" thus encourages us to see ourselves within nature's "greater domain." Indeed, Komunyakaa would have us "see our own reflections in every ritual" (p. 111). Although this call to recognize our place in nature suggests a romantic worldview, one that might, like the Agrarian's worldview, obscure the politics of place, Komunyakaa does not let us rest in such romanticism. He asks us to consider a deeper implication of our connectedness to the natural world, that is, that we cannot damage this fabric of connections "without wounding ourselves" (p. 111).

Komunyakaa's sophisticated understanding of Southern place is also evident in *Magic City* (1992), a collection of poems in which he conjures up the intricacies of his childhood in Bogalusa and the place-specific origins of his poetic vision. Though, in his literary homecoming, the poet immerses himself in memories of his youth, he eschews the nostalgia and sentimentality that often lure us into such ventures. Komunyakaa's poems, therefore, capture the emotional complexity necessary for thinking the depth of Southern place in all its mutations.

In "The Whistle," for example, the speaker works through the "aftershock" of his father's fight with a white lumberyard foreman. The poem first depicts the rich fabric of quotidian life and symbolizes the racism lurking within it: how "something dead under the foundation" of our civil society, the supposed death of racism itself, resurrects the appetites of secret predators that live off a decaying corpse. Perhaps the effort to conceal racism only heightens the desire to bring it back to life. As Komunyakaa (1992) expresses it: "blue jays & redbirds / Wove light through leaves / & something dead under the foundation / Brought worms to life" (p. 3). The poet then shows how the terror of racism fully invades the textures of place experience: "A brick fell into the livingroom like a black body, / & a riot of drunk curses / Left the gladioli & zinnias / Maimed" (p. 5). Finally,

Komunyakaa depicts an awakening to the spirit of resistance and an effort to understand the connectedness of personal experience, place, and history:

> The steel-gray evening was a canvas
> Zigzagged with questions
> Curling up from smokestacks, as dusky birds
> Brushed blues into a montage
> Traced back to *L'Amistad* & the psychosis
> Behind *Birth of a Nation.*
> With eyes against glass & ears to diaphanous doors,
> I heard a cornered prayer.
> (Komunyakaa, 1993, p. 4)

In his home and Southern place, where the pathology of white racism invades the private recesses of black experience, Komunyakaa seeks not solace but a rigorous engagement with the psychosocial complexity of the milieu. Moreover, he conceives of such engagement as the reconstruction and rehistoricizing of place. This is evidenced in the essay "More Than a State of Mind," a brief reflection in which Komunyakaa describes the influence of Southern place on his thought and poetics. Commenting on his affinity with the white Southern writer Lillian Smith, Komunyakaa (2002a) writes:

> I believe each of us internalizes a landscape composite of myths and stories, and we carry that psychological terrain within us as we make our way through the world . . . an overlay by which the future is often colored and through which it is often perceived. However, like Lillian Smith . . . some of us attempt to refashion that inherited landscape through consciousness. (p. 163)

Uncannily, Komunyakaa's remark confirms the idea that initiates this study, which is that place is structurally psychological; it is a space that exists in the mind, and in memory. As his work in *Magic City* reveals, Komunyakaa's effort to refashion an internalized Southern landscape involves an exploration of the intricacies of place experience. We might think of this process in terms of Gaston Bachelard's notion of "topoanalysis," a term introduced in my interdisciplinary review of place. To reiterate, Bachelard describes topoanalysis as "the systematic psychological study of the localities of our intimate lives" (quoted in Casey, 1997, p. 288). Elaborating on Bachelard's important contribution to the conceptualization of place, Casey (1997) challenges us to grasp autobiographical meaning outside the "durational flow" of life (p. 289). "To come to terms with the inner life,"

Casey explains, "it is not enough to constitute a biography or autobiography in narrative terms; one must also, and more crucially, do a topoanalysis of the places one has inhabited or experienced" (p. 289).

Working in this way, through the lived experience of place and outside a linear life narrative, Komunyakaa finds the time of history ("Traced back to *L'Amistad*") and the time of cultural representation ("the psychosis / Behind *Birth of a Nation*") collapsed into subjective *topoi* or places ("diaphanous doors" and "a cornered prayer"). Komunyakaa's return to place does not exclude the significance of time but rather opens subjectivity to the complexity of the past. As Bachelard succinctly explains: "In its countless alveoli space contains compressed time" (quoted in Casey, 1997, p. 289). Self-analysis directed toward the experience of place, therefore, can promote understanding of the way one internalizes diverse and conflicting histories.

If Komunyakaa foregrounds place, how then does he pursue the transformation of place within subjectivity? He does so, I believe, by sustaining ambivalent contact with Southern place. In "More Than a State of Mind," Komunyakaa (2002b) discusses his relationship to Southern place, highlighting his ambivalence toward the region:

> Coming of age [in the South], I was fully aware of both the natural beauty and the social terror surrounding me. The challenge became to acknowledge and resist this terror. My early emotional life grew into the kind of questions that lead men to ponder philosophy and psychology, eventually guiding me to poetry. I became aware of the troublesome contradictions in my town. (p. 163)

In "Dark Waters," Komunyakaa (2002a) further articulates his negotiation of paradox and contradiction. The poems in *Magic City*, he explains, both depict the landscape in which he once found great solitude—"the engine of [his] imagination"—and "present how toxicity taints the social and natural landscape" (pp. 101–102). At the foundation of Komunyakaa's attempt to subjectively reconstruct Southern place, therefore, is a thoroughgoing effort to hold ambivalence toward this region that both nurtures and poisons its people.

If place is pedagogy, as Doll (2000) suggests, then an effort to hold ambivalence in and toward a place rife with a racist history not yet grappled with, or worked through, is itself a powerful teacher. The capacity to hold ambivalence, the psychoanalyst Wilfred Bion maintains, is a necessary and foundational condition for thought (Britzman, 2003; Hoggett & Thompson, 2002). As Deborah Britzman (2003) explains:

> [Bion] argues that thinking is a process of claiming adventure of emotional significance, even if this journey leaves one uncertain and vulnerable. Thus for Bion, thinking is not equated to intellectualization, a cognition devoid of phantasy, or an assumption of the mind/body split. Instead, it is tied to and embroiled in language. (p. 100)

Furthermore, Britzman continues, "the difficulty of thinking thoughts prepares how language is used within groups" (p. 100). A refusal to hold ambivalence, individually or collectively, therefore, can leave us mired in "basic assumptions that unconsciously bind the group and foreclose its capacity to acknowledge its resistance to ideas and change" (p. 100). Paul Hoggett and Simon Thompson (2002) explain Bion's work in the context of communities that run "the risk of being overwhelmed by paranoid anxieties"—communities, for example, made up of racial factions and harboring racist histories (p. 120). In these circumstances, they explain, "the task is to create a forum where different groups can bring their fears, resentments, and perhaps initially their hatreds, to a space where they can be contained and thereby transformed" (p. 120).

In a South dominated by whites who refuse to consider how racist history lives within the present, Komunyakaa's holding of ambivalence is a powerful pedagogical confrontation with the color line. He demonstrates that the language of Southern place can help us bear experience of and thought about the racial traumas that have been absorbed into our social and psychic landscapes. And he teaches us, most importantly, that as we confront and work through the toxicity that place contains, we have an opportunity to reshape the places and worlds we share.

Reshaping the Subject of Southern Place

> I had begun to feel a pull—like gravity, maybe, whatever it is that makes one sure the world is the best planet we have and that one's own part of it is a necessary spiritual terrain, as much one's own as a cast in the eye—that drew me southward again.
>
> —Ellen Douglas (1979/1994, p. 57)

In the novel *The Rock Cried Out,* Ellen Douglas (1979/1994) characterizes the act of writing about place as an encounter with unconscious personal and cultural histories. The novel's narrator and protagonist, Alan McLaurin, writes about his Southern homeplace and conceives of that writing as a search for self in nature, as the romantic poet's act of "inviting the soul." A liberal white man, Alan hopes to secure a sense of identity by poeticizing the Southern landscape and life in the rural South. Place however speaks through Alan in ways that disrupt his effort to pin place down. As he explores the natural environment, rural labor, and small town community relations, the particularities of place that compel him to write prove to be connected with narratives that *unsettle* rather than *secure* his sense of identity, specifically narratives that implicate him in the Southern racism of which he considers himself innocent. Alan's writing about place thus exceeds his conscious grasp, challenging his conception of place as stable aesthetic and personal ground, and registering the indeterminate and culturally complex role place plays in the formation of subjectivity.

Like Kenan, McKnight, and Komunyakaa, Douglas (1979/1994) appropriates tropes from Southern literary history to destabilize the dominant conception of Southern place. Moreover, in *The Rock Cried Out,* she responds to the Southern Renascence tradition directly, challenging "southern renascence constructions of southern history and the Fugitive/Agrarian construction of a unified South as a position of purity and authenticity from which to critique the modern world" (S. Harrison, 2003, p. 4). Working through the desire for an inviolable and innocent subject position at the foundation of Southern place, Douglas foregrounds and undermines its primary supporting figure, the Southern white man relating to the land. Moreover, Douglas reveals the transformation of this figure—the disruption of his attachments to purity and authenticity—through the vicissitudes of his writing life. The close-up on her protagonist's writing life provides a means for conceptualizing autobiographical curriculum inquiry committed to social change in the American South. In the remainder of this chapter, I examine Douglas's novel and describe the dimensions of autobiographical inquiry her novel suggests.

When the novel begins, Alan has left Boston where he worked in a sugar factory and has returned to his home in the rural Mississippi territory of Chickasaw Ridge. From the outset, we find tension between Alan's experience of place and his writing. His Southern homecoming, Alan imagines, is a vehicle through which he can tap the poetic language inside him. He believes he can regain through writing a sense of place he has lost in the din and jumble of city life. This is analogous to the famous speech Wordsworth makes in "Tintern Abbey" in which time spent in London necessitates a return to his more genial spirits, the recovery of the landscape of the past, and emotions associated with home. Speaking of his time in Boston, Alan explains, "I believed I was a poet and was sure my brain was teeming with poems my ears couldn't catch for the traffic noises outside my window in Roxbury and the roar of machinery at the Israel Putnam Sugar

Company, Inc" (Douglas, 1979/1994, p. 9). In his homecoming, Alan seeks a rejuvenated relationship with an internal language, a language not diminished by the tenuousness of the northeastern place in which he has lived. Alan takes the features of Southern place he most remembers to be the constitutive elements of this severed subjective language. When he arrives home, therefore, he attempts to establish his writing life in a pastoral aesthetic that he counterposes to his perception of the North.

Alan intends to recover a sense of self through a sense of place, to mine his Southern roots and affinities for subjective ground. Alan thus idealizes Chickasaw Ridge, land his family owns, as a site of natural beauty and spiritual renewal. While in Boston contemplating his return, he dreams of

> wintry woods—of the pervasive smell . . . of cedar and pine: of smilax and jasmine twisting dark green up into the bare dogwood and walnut and cherry trees; of oaks under shawls of gray moss that turn out when you look closely to be throbbing with pale green life; of the wintry silence, above all, broken only by the voices of birds that stay with us all year. (Douglas, 1979/1994, p. 10)

When referring to his Southern home, Alan earnestly uses "the language of landscape," believing, as does Anne Whiston Spirn (1998), that such language "recovers the dynamic connection between place and those who dwell there" (p. 17). Alan intends to look into the depths of his homeplace and find vibrant meaning in the same way he has discovered life in the gray moss covering old oaks.

In the Southern place that reared him, Alan seeks a reawakening of his being. He describes his journey home as "fleeing the city and dreaming of solitude and inviting my soul" (Douglas, 1979/1994, p. 10). Though his political philosophy differs from that of his conservative agrarian forebears, like them, Alan believes place holds the promise of oneness, transcendence, and moral righteousness. Place secures his belief that "purity [is] possible," that "he could pay his dues from time to time and live, by the light of his convictions, an untroubled, perhaps even a heroic, life" (p. 53). Alan longs for "the romance of life in the country—building, sowing, gathering, [and] observing," and he anticipates the "days and nights that [will] bring on the wings of February storms the poems he [knows] must be waiting to surface, if only he were quiet and patient enough to invite them" (p. 53).

This effort to ground the self in writing about place proves to be a painful and overdetermined process. As an effort to secure stability, the writing task Alan takes up actually excludes or resists knowledge, exposing knowledge as always incomplete, and fortifying a psychical carapace that ensures he will suffer a destabilizing return of the repressed. His writing promotes insularity rather than historical understanding and ultimately stumbles upon traumatic and repressed personal, familial, and cultural narratives.

Alan's vision of identity, place, and creativity cannot hold sway when faced with the cultural complexity of Southern place. Though he returns home for the land's rejuvenating powers, Alan discovers instead its profound ambiguity, and he must confront in his home the disturbing histories and memories that shadow his identity and thought. Resituating himself in Chickasaw, Alan learns of a long concealed interracial love affair in his family, that his family has been complicit in the dispossession of his black neighbors, and that racial hatred motivated the murder of his childhood love. Significantly, his experience of being disturbed by this new knowledge is expressed in terms of a destabilized landscape.

When his Aunt Leila tells him the story of a love affair that she had with a black tenant farmer, Alan explains, "she handed me with it the job of finding someplace to put it down where the weight of it wouldn't tilt Chickasaw so steeply that we would all slide right off the ridge into the ravine" (Douglas, 1979/1994, p. 138). His new knowledge creates "a very real sensation of movement—as if the house and everybody and everything in it shifted along a fault" (p. 124). Reflecting on his gradual awakening to the deeply embedded racial politics of his home, Alan writes: "I feel mostly wonder at how our lives move, by twists and turns, as a creek moves, rippling in its bed, doubling around and shaping itself against the contours of rock and silt and fallen log, eating out a bank and appearing one day, after a rainstorm, flowing down a ravine that yesterday was half a mile from its course" (p. 124). These passages reveal Douglas's effort "to allow the landscape to reassert itself" against stereotypes of Southern place (Jones, 2002, p. 134). She uses the language of the landscape as an inscription of Alan's particular and changing subjective experience of the region, showing that Alan's physical surroundings guide him in a conversation with a history of race relations he has long avoided.

Having longed for total knowledge of place, knowledge that would extricate him from responsibility for the region's politics, Alan feels acutely "the urge of the storyteller to tie up loose ends . . . the urge of the moralist to make his point, [and the urge] of both to give the tale a shape" (Douglas, 1979/1994, p. 302). But he discovers through his writing process and the vicissitudes of the environment that "the shape is still changing," and that even "the dead—[do not] have a finished shape . . . the dead, crumbling to the earth." Thus, in Alan's mutable language of place, the landscape begins to manifest not only the movement of subjective experience but also the presence of lives past. As Alan writes, "Next year the dead will be flaming in the April trees" (pp. 302–303).

Here Douglas captures what Robert Pogue Harrison (2003) calls the "indwelling of the dead in the worlds of the living" (p. x). Identifying the brilliance, perhaps the conflagration, of past lives in our present world, Douglas asks us to continually reshape our relationship to the history we so often ignore even as it blazes in our minds. Through Alan's perspective and crisis of place, she returns us to the question of the dead and how we act out, and might work through, the demands they make on the present. Harrison, too, reminds us of the call of the dead: "We inherit their obsessions; assume their burdens; carry on their causes; promote their mentalities, ideologies, and very often their superstitions; and often we die trying to vindicate their humiliations" (p. x). Though this is an uncertain inheritance, it cannot be refused. *The Rock Cried Out* teaches us that only by acknowledging and resymbolizing our subjection to the past will we create worlds that do not replay the violence the dead have enacted and suffered.

Autobiographical Dimensions of Southern Place

Being-in-place is being-in-language, a writerly act entangled in the skeins of history and our inner lives. In the character of Alan McLaurin, we see that one's perspective on the landscape can obscure the past and one's relationship to others, while it can also become a medium for constructing a more complex autobiography, one that acknowledges lives and histories suppressed by a more romanticized and less culpable vision of place. Alan's autobiographical project and thus his language of place are wrought with the tension of other voices, the voices of black and white men and women subjected to and working through their own particular experiences of the South's racial inheritance. Douglas registers these voices as necessary though unsettling to the sense of self-understanding that Alan pursues. The novel therefore represents not only the undoing of Alan's pastoral ideal and his attempt at reconstructing the self to which it was bound but also the discursive complexity of an autobiographical process that addresses, from a position of whiteness, the history of race in the region.

The Rock Cried Out dislodges the white male Southern writer from his secure Southern place and, in doing so, exposes dimensions of autobiography that, when taken into account, leave the matter of Southern place an unsettled subject. Corresponding with three periods in Alan's life, these autobiographical dimensions also exhibit the three registers of the Lacanian subject. I summarize them as they appear in the narrative to suggest their relevance for social-psychoanalytic inquiry.

In 1964, when Alan is a child, a car crash kills his cousin Phoebe and the wife of his black friend and neighbor Sam Daniels. Years later Alan discovers the crash to have been the result of Ku Klux Klan activity involving friends and family. As a writer exploring the significance of his childhood, therefore, Alan confronts Southern place as the site of traumatic events and intractable memories. And he subsequently attributes to place the power of trauma to shatter language, meaning, and the self.

In psychoanalysis, a trauma is a point of obsessive attachment or fixation, what Lacan theorizes in terms of the Real. Thinking of the Real as a dimension of autobiographical inquiry challenges us to consider the dynamic of fixation in our self-analysis, and to explore new linguistic relationships to experiences that resist symbolization, "language being that which allows for substitution and displacement—the very antithesis of fixation" (Fink, 1995, p. 26). Mark Bracher (2006) describes this process as a "rectification with the real," which "involves coming to recognize that one's own actions, based on motives (identity needs) that one may know nothing of, have served to produce a situation that one consciously wants to prevent" (p. 136). *The Rock Cried Out* exemplifies this process. Throughout the novel, Alan is fixated on moments in his past, unable to grasp the traumatic origins of his confusion about place and identity; however, at the end of the novel, he begins to recognize that his own need for subjective stability compelled him to seek an inviolable sense of place, even as that fantasy concealed the history of violence and racism he consciously wanted to understand and denounce.

The second autobiographical dimension from which Alan derives the meaning of place relates to his romanticization of homeplace and ancestry. This dimension corresponds with Lacan's notion of the Imaginary, a register in which "our central desire . . . is to maintain our sense of bodily integrity and unity in the face of otherness" (Bracher, 2000, p. 156).

In 1971, Alan returns from a foray into the Northeast to rediscover his Southern roots. He is hopeful that the Southern landscape and natural environment will inspire his poetic sensibilities. As a romantic poet, Alan seeks stable ground for the self in the concreteness and natural beauty of Southern place. He therefore attributes to place, narcissistically, those aspects of himself he wants to confirm and secure: moral virtue, spiritual depth, and intellectual plenitude. As a force in autobiographical inquiry, the Imaginary opposes any threat to the ego, allowing the ego to find its mirror image in nonthreatening aspects of the external world. The Imaginary dimension splits the world, positioning others as either a threat or a source of comfort, figures of identification or rivalry. Providing the ego a sense of unity or totality and obscuring one's internal otherness, the Imaginary also forestalls a rectification with the real.

As Alan learns about the events of his youth and the complex racial politics of his homeplace, he becomes aware that his poetic intentions repress rather than excavate the complexity of Southern place. Years after his idealized homecoming, he explains that the romantic poetics of his earlier life denied "what was going on around [him] . . . the pattern it cried out for" (Douglas, 1979/1995, p. 12). This awareness engenders a third distinctive relationship to place, an autobiographical dimension we can understand in terms of Lacan's Symbolic register, which contains the "master signifiers" and "knowledge systems" that give meaning to our identities (Bracher, 2000, pp. 149–151).

In 1978, Alan reflects on the events of 1964 and 1971 that have shattered his idealism about Southern place and his conception of himself as a writer. He has not, however, relinquished his attention to the particularities of place. Instead, he has begun to expand his conception of the language and writing life that might allow the marginalized histories of Southern place to surface. As an autobiographer, Alan explores Southern place as a complex field of social and historical meanings. This field of meanings is represented in the many "embedded narratives, confessions, and delayed revelations" that constitute the novel and that expose historical through lines from slavery and the civil rights movement to the race and gender politics of the characters' everyday lives (S. Harrison, 2003, p. 13). Alan discovers he does not have a definitive, secure position in this social symbolic network. In this mode of thought, Alan attributes to place a significance that can be only partially grasped, acknowledging an excess of meaning associated with the Symbolic order. Through Alan's struggle to write, therefore, we witness an intractable system of narratives that contribute to self-formation. This system of narratives, Mark Bracher (2006) explains, "range[s] from chronicles of one's moment-by-moment activity to the broad sweep of one's entire (though often largely tacit) autobiography and ultimately to the history of the cosmos and one's place in it" (p. 17).

For Alan, working through these dimensions of place exacerbates a paradox and therefore the pain of writing. As the writer strives to shape a discontinuous and endlessly unfolding world, his writing excludes meanings that ultimately subtend what a writer creates. Alan has suffered in the face of this paradox, he eventually realizes, because he has desired a position of utter virtue from which he can witness and write through the traumas of the past, a faultless position whose impossibility his writing inevitably exposes.

In Alan's struggle to write, we see his effort to understand his own endlessly shifting place in a social symbolic world. Place in this narrative, therefore, signifies the unconscious play of language in one's experience. Rather than valuing an "autochthonous ideal," Douglas promotes an understanding of Southern place as both a force of exclusion and an embodiment of desire, a point of identification and a source of trauma. Instead of fetishizing Southern place, she charts a process of confronting place, including one's singular place in language, a process that can inform autobiographical inquiry conducted for the purpose of developing social-psychoanalytic insight.

Language belongs to no one individual. It is a collective homeland and a space of individual exile. A space of the living and a site of buried histories and meanings. Burial, in this sense, "means to store, preserve, and put the past on hold" (R. P. Harrison, 2003, p. xi). Through language, then, we harbor fragments of a past waiting to emerge. Harrison writes: "Dead etymons, latent meanings, and lateral connotations lie buried in the roots and phonemes of our living words, where they carry an active afterlife. Our psyches are the graveyards of impressions, traumas, desires, and archetypes that confound the law of obsolescence" (2003, p. xi).

The otherness of language itself threatens Alan's identity. He tries to assuage this threat through a romanticized poetics of place. The subjective position he attempts to fortify through this poetics is one in which he can acknowledge the South's history of racism and racial violence while not subjectivizing it, that is, while not grasping this history within the contours of his self-concept. However, the capacity to grasp Southern history in this way, to figure it as an influence on the formation of subjectivity is *necessary* for the construction of Southern places that do not remain enthralled to the region's historical trauma or bound by the narcissistic projections of those in positions of cultural dominance. In Alan McLaurin's "rectification with the real," therefore, we witness the opening and reshaping of the subject of Southern place. In contrast to the Agrarians, who encouraged us to find in the landscape a selfsame identity, Douglas does not provide us an imitable autobiographical method or process. She does however disclose the dimensions of an interminable process of self-creation, as she invites us to explore and expand the contours of our own particular places in the world.

CONCLUSION

Indeterminate Ground

In the essay "Where is Bynam Woods?" Ellen Douglas (2004) writes: "We will have great difficulty understanding or putting to use our past, as long as we persist in tearing apart all the visible, palpable evidence that we have been here" (p. 21). Douglas's essay, included in her volume *Witnessing,* urges us toward another consideration of the significance and power of Southern place. She frames this conversation through her own experience of place, remembering a now-razed old-growth forest she saw as she traveled in the 1930s between Alexandria and Natchitoches, Louisiana. She remembers Bynam Woods specifically to reflect on the meaning of its destruction. "Sometime shortly after the Second World War," she writes, "I drove that way again. The woods were gone: giant live oaks, the pines as big around as silos and as tall as the Guaranty Bank building in Alexandria, the forest floor, deep in humus, blossoming with trillium in the spring—thousands of three-pointed stars—and climbing yellow jasmine, dogwoods, and redbuds. All were gone. Not one tree remained" (p. 17).

The destruction of Bynam Woods through industrial growth in the region represents for Douglas (2004) not only an enormous disregard for the natural environment but also a woeful drive to cleanse individual and collective memory. Douglas interrogates a national and regional "capacity . . . to destroy places," exposing the way we "erase from our minds, from our land . . . the memory of our past constructions, our past triumphs, our past errors" (p. 19). She witnesses how "our past vanishes" as we "grade off the face of the landscape and create a new one" (p. 19). And she asks us to resist the "incurable innocence" that prevents us from confronting the past and place we have inherited (p. 18). Fully engaging the region's agrarian literary tradition, Douglas also vigorously critiques the traditional notion of Southern place as the ground of purity, thus calling us to the difficult emotional and intellectual labor of working through the past this ideology represses.

Writing this book has involved me in such a process of working-through. Through Southern literature, I have investigated our capacity to forget the past in the name of purity, to deny desire in the name of identity, and to destroy place in the name of cultural ideals. Studying a cultural belief in the purity of place has helped me recognize and question my own need for a secure sense of place. And it has helped me bear witness to the creation of new places in language, places that expand my vision of self and society, places open to possibilities of subjective movement and social change.

For me, this book fosters political hope. For many of my readers, however, the transference evident in my autobiographical inquiry may threaten to overshadow the vision of social justice that has inspired the work. This tension invites me to consider its relevance and meaning for the curriculum of place I've presented. By way of a conclusion, I elaborate on my own process of working-through, showing how the foregoing chapters and autobiographical interludes address the tension between repeating and transcending the past.

A process of working-through, LaCapra (1997) argues, does not wholly transcend the "acting-out" that is an unconscious return to past disturbances or losses. Acting-out and working-through are "intimately linked" (p. 82), as the former provides the material to be interpreted and explored in various realms of lived experience. The two processes are nonetheless distinguishable. "To act out a transferential relation," LaCapra explains, "is to compulsively repeat the past as if it were fully present, to relive it typically in a manic or melancholic manner" (p. 89). "To work through problems," on the other hand, "requires acknowledging them" (p. 89). LaCapra furthers the definition of working-through, naming both the repetition and the social milieu that are necessary for the process. Working-through, he explains,

> involves an attempt to counteract the tendency to deny, repress or blindly repeat [problems], and it enables one to acquire critical perspective allowing for a measure of control and responsible action, notably including a mode of repetition related to the renewal of life in the present. It also requires an interactive context that mitigates isolation, depression and melancholy—a context that may have to extend beyond both self-reflection and a one-on-one relationship such as that between analyst and analysand or writer and reader. (pp. 89–90)

In keeping with LaCapra's definition, Seth Moglen (2005) argues that to foster political hope and social change, working-through (or mourning) must not only acknowledge the subjects and objects of loss but also "identify the social forces that have produced any particular experience of collective loss," opening "the question of the variable relationships that exist between and among those forces, the bereaved, and that which has been lost" (p. 158).

Emphasizing social context and a creative return to a psychical impasse, these accounts of working-through illuminate my research process. In the interlude "A Nascent Language about Our Shared World," I explored the way a specific place both affords me a sense of personal meaning and unsettles my understanding of family and self-identity. I described my own deep attachment to place, suggesting a repetition or blockage precluding insight into my experience. However, reading this attachment through a work of Southern literature prompted me to acknowledge the emotional impasse. And the acknowledgment, finally, provided the groundwork for further interpretation of my personal language of place.

In Chapter 1, "The American South: Subjective and Social Terrain," I followed the psychoanalyst's call to locate subjective experience in multiple contexts, elaborating on the psychosocial milieu of the South that encompasses and infuses my perception of place. Just as my autobiographical narrative revealed unconscious self/other dynamics at work in my experience of place, my investigation of an overdetermined conception of place in Southern literature exposed a cultural denial of the region's racist past and present. A theoretical account of the social foundations of subjectivity then helped frame my effort to connect individual and collective processes of working-through. Finally, to enable the analysis of my own subjective positioning in white patriarchal culture, I reviewed the historical foundations of white Southern identity.

In the interlude "The Language of the Landscape," I described the difficulty of my personal effort to find an "interactive context that mitigates isolation" (LaCapra, 1997, p. 90). If my narrative about my father demonstrates the power of an impasse in my experience of white male identity, it also serves as a mode of repetition dedicated to renewal of life in the present. A repetition becomes a blockage, LaCapra explains, when one develops "a mimetic relation to the past which is represented or relived as if it were fully present rather than represented in memory and inscription" (p. 81). In this section, I explored a language of the landscape, one imbued with a difficult history, to demonstrate my ongoing effort to grasp the vicissitudes of remembering and rearticulating the past.

In Chapter 2, "Southern Place: Autochthony, White Masculinity, and Southern Aberrations," I identified more specifically the social forces that have produced, and prevented acknowledgment of, violence and racism in the South. The autochthonous ideal, a form of cultural compensation for a white male sense of insufficiency, represents what LaCapra (1997) calls a "generalization of trauma and victimage" (p. 84). I analyzed the work of the Nashville Agrarians, Donald Davidson specifically, revealing how, in Southern history and culture, the losses of white men have displaced the suffering of women and black men. This displacement has been so profound that attempts to respond to the suffering of those who are marginalized appear as aberrations or crises of Southern place. To situate these concerns in my personal process of working-through, in the interlude entitled "Questioning Homewardness," I described how romantic strains of Southern literature and culture have become embedded in my own thought and writing.

In Chapter 3, "The Strange Limbo of Southern Place," I brought focus to the psychical impasse that grounds conventional white masculinity in the South. My analysis of two contemporary narratives seems, perhaps, to afford me personal distance from the questions of race, gender, and sexuality that I explore. More accurately, however, this analysis represents what LaCapra calls "re-petitioning . . . for critical distance" (p. 81). Randall Kenan's "Run, Mourner, Run" and Reginald McKnight's "The White Boys" allow me to attend more closely to the aspects of white masculinity that I raise in the foregoing personal narratives. As Kenan and McKnight depict the psychological entanglements of Southern white men, and the consequences of a white male anxiety of insufficiency, these writers enable me to critique race and gender dynamics that infuse my experience and identity. My autobiography is implied rather than explicit in this chapter, though it nonetheless compels the analysis and working-through.

The stories in Chapter 3 expose unconscious dynamics of the hegemonic white male Southern subject. "Run, Mourner, Run" (the title itself suggesting a melancholic impasse) presents a white male disavowal of interracial and homosexual relationships as the impediment to a process of social-psychoanalysis in the South. Kenan himself, however, refigures the Southern land as a vehicle for self-analysis and social understanding. Though he presents the land as a symbol of marred relationships to self and other, relationships the conventional white male subject refuses to acknowledge and explore, Kenan also suggests the possibility of a deepened intimacy and communication between men, white and black. However tragic the story's outcome, the sensuality and communication

Kenan portrays provide hope for reversing the process by which the dominant conception of Southern place is formed.

Like Kenan, Reginald McKnight provides a means for rethinking both Southern place and the construction of white male identity. Moreover, McKnight teaches us that when traumatic histories go unacknowledged, these histories wreak havoc on memory and relationships. "The White Boys" suggests that history travels through secrets, haunts gestures, and invades our slightest perceptions of place. The story ultimately emphasizes the subtle ways our lives are interwoven with history and calls us to confront racism in our everyday lives.

In the interlude entitled "Opening the Landscape to Questions of Identity and History," I attempted to create an interactive narrative context, one that demonstrates my effort to situate the region's history in my enigmatic, subjective experience. Chapter 4, "Reshaping Our Inherited Landscape," extended my effort to locate traces of history in private language and experience. I investigated the work of two contemporary writers who reconceptualize the traditional notion of Southern place, writers who emphasize the power of place to present us with social conditions we have ignored or obscured. For Yusef Komunyakaa and Ellen Douglas, Southern place is ground for understanding the way "one's deep needs collide with the social structures in which one lives" (Moglen, 2005, p. 164). Komunyakaa (2002b) pursues the transformation of place within subjectivity, naming the social terror that must be worked through if one is to contribute to the renewal of the South. His poetry invites us to confront the toxicity of the regional landscape as we attempt to refashion that landscape in consciousness.

At the end of Chapter 4, I turned to the work of Ellen Douglas (1979/1994), specifically drawing on a narrative, *The Rock Cried Out*, that resonates deeply with my own inquiry into Southern place. *The Rock Cried Out* portrays an interdependence between language and place, one that I discovered in my reflections on home and the rural South. The main character of the novel, Alan McLaurin, explores a similar nexus only to have the history and politics of the South threaten to upend his writing life and autobiographical understanding. In response, Alan attempts to fully ground the self, to totalize it, in writing about home and the rural landscape. Such an effort, LaCapra (1997) argues, remains enthralled to a "phantasm of total mastery, [and] full ego-identity," precluding the creation of "a desirable democratic identity in the present" (LaCapra, 1997, pp. 82, 95). Alan's writing process, therefore, proves to be painful and overdetermined. When taken up as an effort to secure white male subjectivity, his writing excludes or resists knowledge. It creates insularity rather than historical understanding and becomes entangled in, rather than promoting insight into, traumatic personal, familial, and cultural narratives.

In this novel, however, Ellen Douglas portrays not only the melancholic impasse of a white male Southern writer but also his complex process of working-through. Ultimately, Alan begins to move beyond merely acknowledging the South's history of racism and racial violence to grasping this history within the contours of his self-concept. He comes to understand that his life and writing are endlessly taking shape, as they are preinhabited by those who came before him.

Thus, unlike the Nashville Agrarians, Douglas does more than regret the destruction of place. She descends into the debris to find a place from which to speak, and she calls for the recreation of place through language and inquiry. In *Witnessing,* Douglas (2004) urges us to "take possession of our personal pasts [and] our history" through intellectual labor, through "the slow, delightful, and laborious process of *rereading* a great novel, of *memorizing* a poem, of meditating on, learning the history and observing the consequences of behavior, [of studying] these demanding human disciplines [that] are essential to becoming a whole human being" (p. 26, emphasis in original).

By reclaiming our personal and collective histories in writing, Douglas (2004) explains, we create "imaginary countries" capable of subverting those that perpetuate social injustice (p. 113). Such writing is often painful and difficult, requiring that we dismantle the problematic images and ideologies we inherit. We see this as Douglas writes about Natchez, Mississippi, a Southern place bound up with clichés and myths, with images of "moonlights and magnolias and hoopskirts and aristocrats and mint juleps—the very essence of horrible romance" (p. 113). We work through such overdetermined images, Douglas explains, because "we try for detachment," and the creation of worlds to replace "those that exist as products of someone else's corrupt imaginings" (p. 113).

AUTOBIOGRAPHICAL CONCLUSION

The Limits and Liminality of Place

I grew up in the suburban South of the 1970s and 1980s, where the white middle class carved neighborhoods from a shrinking natural landscape. The neighborhood in which I lived stretched across a hardy terrain of South Louisiana creeks and woods, capturing at its center a segment of wildlife just rich and deep enough to allow me to lose myself in nature, and just small enough to foster my curiosity about the way places connect and overlap, come into being, and come to an end. As a young boy, I explored this small tract of wilderness to its edges. I followed its creeks to their tributaries, hiked and hunted through its marsh and thickets, and ventured through it into imaginary worlds. I ventured through it, that is, until I found myself, a bit dismayed, standing in a neighbor's manicured yard, on the side of the interstate, or in the parking lot of a new Seven-Eleven convenience store. Ending starkly in landscapes of suburban propriety and urban sprawl, these woods, it eventually became clear to me, were a buffer of some kind. They held things out as they held me in.

My experience of this natural landscape has taught me that place plays a complex role in the formation of subjectivity and social identity. This wooded terrain infused my experience of suburbia with a pastoral ideal, with a sense of living close to the land, encouraging an outward journey while keeping me in the vicinity of a secure domestic sphere. But it also invited me to read and learn at the limits of places and experiences, to pursue the limits and liminality of the curriculum that places hold. These woods communicated with other places in my experience, inscribing my consciousness with a range of socially constructed boundaries, boundaries between nature and culture, the suburbs and the city, the private and the public—and therefore, boundaries between femininity and masculinity, the middle class and poor, white and black. If, through its inscription of social difference, this wooded landscape promised protection from the larger social world, I return to it for another reason, specifically to name the gendered and racialized splitting that is enacted in the idealization of such places.

In this book, I have explored the fear of displacement, the fear of moving beyond an experience or conceptualization of place, a fear that binds the meaning of race and gender identity. Autobiographically, I have investigated what it means for my life and identity, as a white Southern man, that I have traversed boundaries between dramatically different places while remaining attached to a conception of place as stable subjective ground. I have investigated what it means that the places I experience—imaginary and real, natural and built, private and social—collide and communicate as I travel between them, becoming active features of my internal world, while I have nonetheless learned to associate the power of place with the protectiveness of home.

When as a child I returned home from the woods, I left a place where I risked getting lost and entered a familial environment whose power rested in its capacity to assuage risk. When I ventured into social spaces—school the most significant among them—I encountered a world beyond my family's substantial protections, yet my sense of self remained moored in a harbor of maternal care. When I confronted the culturally complex social world of South Louisiana, I did so from the security of home, from a feminized space that eclipsed the place significance of other worlds around me. My escape into the woods and return home as well as my grasp of the social sphere were gendered. So were my desire for stability and my capacity for risk. Gendered as well then is my current and developing understanding of place.

A familiar Southern tableau frames the suburban wilderness where I spent much of my youth. In this scene from my childhood, tall oaks covered in Spanish moss line a dark and ominous swamp. And a lush magnolia tree canopies a grassy hill, marking the threshold through which I escaped the banalities of insular community, entered a suburban wildwood, and recovered something of the texture of life's mystery. The magnolia and the mossy oak, therefore, stand sentinel over my earliest memories of the complexity of place. For all my desire to uproot them, to bear witness to a South unmarked by signs of deep investment in white patriarchal culture, these place markers hold firmly to the South as I know and experience it. These and other overdetermined symbols of Southern regional identity have, therefore, taken root in the landscape of my thoughts about the progressive reconstruction of the American South. The South in whose reconstruction I desire to participate must inevitably be the one in which I find myself deeply subjectively invested.

In everyday speech, place represents our unique subjective positioning (my place in the world) as well as the intrinsically bounded, fundamentally cultural, sites or locales with which we interact (Harrison, 2002, p. 350). The notion of place thus circumscribes neither stable identity nor coherent community, but rather an unceasing tension between self and world. If place seems stable, defined as it is "with reference to the apparent immediacy of a lived here-and-now" (Grosz, 1995, p. 93), when we question the meaning of place in our lives, we move through the palpability of place toward the instability at its core. Kaja Silverman (2000) speaks to this instability when she writes: "The experience of being within the 'here and now' is completely ineffable—it defies every kind of symbolization" (p. 39).

Silverman captures the subject's place in language as a lack of spatial and temporal presence. Her purpose is to emphasize the psychical consequences of this lack, that is, that "a lost fullness" founds our place in the world, our desire for connections, and our efforts to create meaning. I refer to this theory of subjectivity to suggest that the meaning we attribute to social and cultural places derives from the experience of loss.

I discover this limit, this sense of loss, in my own autobiographical study of place. And working through this sense of loss has enlivened my writing life. My immediate surroundings and my memory of places from the past have provided language for an internal journey, allowing me to render complex experiences before I fully understand them, and compelling me to write without the security of certainty. Through this writing, I've become more aware of the metaphors of place that govern my sense of identity and community. And I've come to recognize the intermingling of places—such as home, nature, school, and society—where I've expected to find separate spheres of experience.

I study place to conceptualize curriculum as a venue for social change in the South. This work has involved me in analysis of the regional specificity of forms of social hatred. And it has challenged me to consider the way social violence is embedded in Southern culture, perpetuated through cultural fantasy, and internalized by individuals in positions of cultural dominance. Through my study of Southern place, I have questioned my own privilege as a white man. As I've challenged my own position, I've also sought a relationship to place in my experience that would provide the narrative foundation for criticizing the reactionary politics of the region.

As I've shown, the study of place can illuminate the way we inhabit simultaneously a subjective and a social world. Our autobiographies of place can help us rethink and reintegrate divided spheres of experience: public/private, worldly/domestic, male/female, and black/white. They can create opportunities for examining subjective displacement—alienation and retreat—from public and private realms. They can, therefore, teach us how we derive a sense of connectedness to and agency in the social sphere and how we might communicate with estranged and unconscious aspects of the self. Within a social-psychoanalytic framework, we pursue social connectedness and self-communication not as social assimilation and self-adjustment, but in an effort to contribute to the progressive reconstruction of our private and public worlds.

NOTES

1. Thrownness is a concept from Heidegger's phenomenology that expresses our being in a situation whose origin, reason, or destination cannot be known. Extending Heidegger's notion to a Lacanian conception of the subject, Kaja Silverman (2000) uses the term "thrownness" to refer to the situatedness of being and subjectivity (p. 35).
2. Kincheloe, Pinar, and Slattery (1994) also theorize this social psychoanalytic process: "The labor of the individual to free himself or herself from a distorted and undermining past has its parallel in the political activity of groups committed to simultaneous social and self critique" (p. 409).
3. An overdetermined sense of place as "white place" certainly has political consequences that exceed the way Southern history and society are intellectually grasped. Two examples demonstrate how white supremacy in the South has been perpetuated through the control and dominance of actual places. In the context of the debate about reparations for African Americans, Raymond Winbush (2003) discusses the racist practice of "whitecapping." A primarily rural Southern phenomenon, whitecapping was the practice by which "night riders confiscat[ed] land from vulnerable Blacks during the era of Jim Crow" (p. 48). In his discussion, Winbush introduces the Associated Press study *Torn from the Land,* which reports on "thousands of Black victims of land takings and the violence associated with the crimes" (p. 53). Associated Press writers Todd Lewan and Dolores Barclay (2001) explain that the AP alone uncovered 107 instances of land theft. In these cases, from 406 black landowners, whites stole more than 24,000 acres of land. Another conjunction of white dominance and land control can be seen in the history of my hometown, Baton Rouge, Louisiana. David Goldfield (2002) uses Baton Rouge to explain how, through municipal land annexation, white politicians have diluted black votes. Through the 1960s and 1970s Baton Rouge annexed large outlying white populations into a city that would have been "nearly half black by 1980" (p. 259). In the 1970s, when a black population requested to be incorporated into the city, the city began to slow its annexation practice. "In 1980 white civic leaders in Baton Rouge revived a plan to abolish the city council and expand the parish (county) council to take jurisdiction over the city" (p. 259). As of the 2000 Census, East Baton Rouge Parish was 56% white and 40% black, and the metro area of Baton Rouge—governed by a predominately white, parish elected council—was 50% black and 45% white.
4. Christopher Bollas (1992) employs the term "self experience" to capture what he calls "the ironic position" of human subjectivity. He explains that "self experience" captures

the distinction and interplay between "the self that experiences" and the "experiencing of our self." In his discussion of this "ambiguity of being that constitutes the human," Bollas emphasizes a point relevant to the question of the way social law infuses personal experience. The human subject, he writes, "experiences himself both as the arranger of life and as the arranged" (p. 27). I find the notion of "self experience" helpful in moving students toward an understanding of the way our individual subjectivities come to form through a social symbolic network.

5. In *Contingency, Hegemony, Universality: Contemporary Dialogues on the Left,* Judith Butler, Ernesto Laclau, and Slavoj Žižek (2000) engage with these questions in a compelling and often contentious dialogue that draws on philosophy, psychoanalysis, and social theory. Much of the debate surrounds Jacques Lacan's concept of "the Real" and its relationship to the social symbolic network(s) we inhabit. Although the Butler, Laclau, and Žižek discussion raises crucial issues about the relationship between subjectivity and the social field, for my purposes it remains too far outside the question of one's articulation of self-experience to aid in my theorization of autobiographical inquiry. Alongside *Contingency, Hegemony, Universality,* therefore, I read another text that foregrounds the question of "the Real." In *World Spectators,* Silverman (2000) brilliantly intermingles Lacanian psychoanalysis and Heideggerian phenomenology to provide a vision of the subject's individuation in a complex social, political, and aesthetic world. Without displacing the concept of the socially constituted subject, Silverman provides an account of the unique "libidinal language" that we are, until death, in the process of constructing.
6. Frosh refers to Michael Rustin's (1991) *The Good Society and the Inner World* and Joel Kovel's (1984) *White Racism.*
7. Discussing the construction of whiteness in the early twentieth century, Grace Hale (1998) writes: "Like other Americans seeking social order, white southerners chose geographic anchors, whether the imagined spaces evoked by narratives or the physical spaces recaptured through spectacle, literally to ground their racial identity within the mobility of modernity. . . . White southerners created their modern sense of themselves as different, externally, from the rest of Americans and different, internally, from African Americans, at the level of culture" (p. 9).
8. The Agrarian's definition of the South as an anti-industrialist region has been profoundly influential, obscuring for many the racism and violence in the South's history and present. A surprising example of this influence can be seen in Eugene Genovese's "embrace of reactionary southern conservatism" (Pinar, 2004, p. 238). Genovese, once a Marxist slave historian, has now turned to the South's agrarian critique of capitalism and technological progress, only to minimize the continuing power of racism in the region. Of the South, he writes, "despite continued temptations and bad moments, their movement shows signs of exorcising the racism that has marred much of its history" (quoted in Pinar, 2004, p. 237). Wholly supporting the myth of Southern graciousness and sincerity, he continues: "[T]he people of the South, across lines of race, class and sex, are as generous, gracious, courteous, decent—in a word, civilized—as any people it has ever been my privilege to get to know" (quoted in Pinar, 2004, p. 237).

9. In his analysis of Southern place in Agrarian thought, Romine (2002) questions the nature of the location that would, according to these writers, allow the emergence of authentic Southern culture and identity. "In short," he asks, "were farms necessary?" (p. 30).
10. Mitchell's account resembles Jacobus's (1999) theory of landscape in fiction, in which landscape provides a relationship to absence and loss.
11. Davidson used the phrase as early as 1933. In an essay titled "Sectionalism in the United States," he describes "powerful research into the past [that] is paralleled by a new sense of place" (quoted in Bone, 2005, p. 28).
12. Lacan uses the term "captate" for this ego function, suggesting both captivation and capture, that is, both the seduction and the imprisonment of the subject by the specular image (Evans, 1996, p. 20).
13. DiPiero (2002, pp. 42–43) borrows the notion of antagonism from Slavoj Žižek, who aligns it with the disturbance of the Real. Antagonism, therefore, exceeds language and is experienced as a failure of meaning.
14. The cultural theories of Annette Kolodny (1975) and Eve Kosofsky Sedgwick (1985) inform my understanding of Kenan's story. The story reveals the gendering of the land as feminine, a white male "pastoral impulse" Kolodny (1975) examines in *The Lay of the Land.* Kolodny argues "land-as-woman" is the "central metaphor of American pastoral experience" (p. 158). As a feminine coded entity, the land bears the effects of the male splitting of the object; it is both nurturing and threatening, "beautiful" and "potentially emasculating" (p. 9). In Kenan's story, the land-as-woman metaphor functions specifically in a way that Sedgwick's (1985) work illuminates. In *Between Men,* she describes man's use of women as a medium of repressed homosexual relationships: "[N]ormative man uses a woman as a conduit of a relationship in which the true *partner* is a man" (Sedgwick, 1985, p. 26). Sedgwick's analysis helps me read the Southern land as a white male projection that mediates socially unacceptable relationships between (white and black) men.
15. In Slavoj Žižek's (1998) phrasing, ideological fantasy is the "publicly unacknowledged 'obscene' supplement" of the "the public, 'official,' ideological texture" (p. 159).
16. Žižek's theory of fantasy parallels Richard King's (1980) account in *A Southern Renaissance: The Cultural Awakening of the American South, 1930–1955.* Discussing the Southern family romance, King explains that fantasy refuses knowledge of the way "we must live in a world with other people." Therefore, though "all cultures are based upon certain fantasies," fantasies of race and gender difference can come to dominate social interactions and perceptions. In such cases, we might say a culture has become fantastic. In my analysis of Southern place, I am concerned with the way white male fantasies continue to bind negotiations of Southern place and community. They do so, in part, by restricting our interrogation of Southern history. "In cultures grown fantastic," King argues, "the regressive or reactionary form of memory is dominant," as such cultures desire "the impossible—repetition—rather than the necessary recollection and working through of the past" (p. 17).
17. Mary Jacobus (1999) argues landscapes confront us with absence and distance.

REFERENCES

Alcorn, M. W. (2002). *Changing the subject in English class: Discourse and the constructions of desire.* Carbondale and Edwardsville: Southern Illinois University Press.

Alexius, N. (2004). From the author. *Country Roads*, 21(6), 61.

Bal, M. (2002). Autotopography: Louise Bourgeois as builder. *Biography: An Interdisciplinary Quarterly*, 25(1), 180–203.

Barry, J. M. (1997). *Rising tide: The great Mississippi flood of 1927 and how it changed America.* New York: Simon and Schuster.

Basso, K. H. (1996). Wisdom sits in places: Notes on a Western Apache landscape. In S. Feld and K. H. Basso (Eds.), *Senses of place* (pp. 13–52). Santa Fe, NM: School of American Research Press.

Bersani, L. (1990). *The culture of redemption.* Cambridge, MA: Harvard University Press.

Beth. (2001). Unpublished student paper. Course: Teaching, Schooling, and Society. Louisiana State University.

Bollas, C. (1992). *Being a character: Psychoanalysis & self experience.* New York: Hill and Wang.

Bollas, C. (2000). Architecture and the unconscious. *International Forum of Psychoanalysis*, 9(1/2), 28–42.

Bone, M. (2003). Were farms necessary: The agrarian question. *Mississippi Quarterly*, 56(3), 421–438.

Bone, M. (2005). *The postsouthern sense of place in contemporary fiction.* Baton Rouge: Louisiana State University Press.

Bracher, M. (1993). *Lacan, discourse, and social change: A psychoanalytic cultural criticism.* Ithaca and London: Cornell University Press.

Bracher, M. (2000). Lacanian psychoanalysis and postmodernism. In A. Elliott and C. Spezzano (Eds.), *Psychoanalysis at its limits: Navigating the postmodern turn* (pp. 145–172). London and New York: Free Association Books.

Bracher, M. (2006). *Radical pedagogy: Identity, generativity, and social transformation.* New York: Palgrave Macmillan.

Britzman, D. P. (1998). *Lost subjects, contested objects: Toward a psychoanalytic inquiry of learning.* Albany: State University of New York Press.

Britzman, D. P. (2003). *After-Education: Anna Freud, Melanie Klein, and psychoanalytic histories of learning.* Albany: State University of New York Press.

Butler, J. (1997). *The psychic life of power: Theories of subjection.* Stanford, CA: Stanford University Press.

Butler, J. (2003). Violence, mourning, politics. *Studies in Gender & Sexuality*, 4(1), 9–37.

Butler, J., Laclau, E., and Žižek, S. (2000). *Contingency, hegemony, universality: Contemporary dialogues on the left.* New York: Verso

Callejo Pérez, D., Fain, S. M., and Slater, J. J. (Eds.) (2004). *Pedagogy of place: Understanding place as a social aspect of education.* New York: Peter Lang.

Casey, E. S. (1993). *Getting back into place: Toward a renewed understanding of the place-world.* Bloomington and Indianapolis: Indiana University Press.

Casey, E. S. (1996). How to get from space to place in a fairly short stretch of time: Phenomenological prolegomena. In S. Feld and K. H. Basso (Eds.), *Senses of place* (pp. 13–52). Santa Fe, NM: School of American Research Press.

Casey, E. S. (1997). *The fate of place: A philosophical history.* Berkeley: University of California Press.

Casey, E. S. (2001). Between geography and philosophy: What does it mean to be in the place-world? *Annals of the Association of American Geographers*, 91(4), 683–693.

Cooper, R. R. (1998, February 1). Affirmative actions. *New York Times Book Review, 147*, 30.

Davidson, D. (1930/1977). A mirror for artists. In *I'll take my stand: The South and the agrarian tradition* (pp. 28–60). Baton Rouge and London: Louisiana State University Press.

Davidson, D. (1938). *Attack on Leviathan: Regionalism and nationalism in the United States.* Chapel Hill: University of North Carolina Press.

Davidson, D. (1957). *Still rebels, still Yankees and other essays.* Baton Rouge: Louisiana State University Press.

Dean, T. (1991). *Gary Snyder and the American unconscious: Inhabiting the ground.* New York: St. Martin's Press.

Dean, T. (2000). The other's voice: Cultural imperialism and poetic impersonality in Gary Snyder's Mountains and Rivers without End. *Contemporary Literature*, 41(3), 462–495.

DeLillo, D. (1982). *The names.* New York: Random House.

Deming, A. H., and Savoy, L. E. (Eds.) (2002). *The colors of nature: Culture, identity, and the natural world.* Minneapolis, MN: Milkweed Editions.

DiPiero, T. (2002). *White men aren't.* Durham, UK: Duke University Press.

Doll, M. A. (2000). *Like letters in running water: A mythopoetics of curriculum.* Mahwah, NJ: Lawrence Erlbaum Associates.

Dollard, J. (1937/1957). *Caste and class in a Southern town.* New York: Doubleday Anchor.

Donaldson, S. V. (1997). Gender, race, and Allen Tate's profession of letters in the South. In A. G. Jones and S. V. Donaldson (Eds.), *Haunted bodies: Gender and Southern texts* (pp. 492–518). Charlottesville, VA and London: University Press of Virginia.

Donaldson, S. V. (1999). Contributing essay. A symposium: The business of inventing the South. *Mississippi Quarterly*, 52(4), 662–669.

Douglas, E. (1979/1994). *The rock cried out.* Baton Rouge: Louisiana State University Press.

Douglas, E. (2004). *Witnessing.* Jackson: University Press of Mississippi.

Dunbar, A. (Ed.) (2004). *Where we stand: Voices of southern dissent.* Montgomery, AL: New South Books.

Edgerton, S. H. (1996). *Translating the curriculum: Multiculturalism and cultural studies.* New York: Routledge.

Eigen, M. (1992). *Coming through the whirlwind. Case studies in psychotherapy.* Wilmette, IL: Chiron Publications.

Evans, D. (1996). *An introductory dictionary of Lacanian psychoanalysis.* New York: Routledge.

Faulkner, W. (1929/1956). *The sound and the fury.* New York: Vintage Books.

Faulkner, W. (1942/1990). *Go down, Moses.* New York: Vintage Books.

Figlio, K., and Richards, B. (2003). The containing matrix of the social. *American Imago,* 60(4), 407–428.

Fink, B. (1995). *The Lacanian subject: Between language and jouissance.* Princeton, NJ: Princeton University Press.

Frosh, S. (1994). *Sexual difference: Masculinity & psychoanalysis.* London and New York: Routledge.

Frosh, S. (2002a). *After words: The personal in gender, culture and psychotherapy.* Basingstoke, UK: Palgrave.

Frosh, S. (2002b). The other. *American Imago,* 59(4), 389–408.

Fuss, D. (1995). *Identification papers.* New York: Routledge.

Gilmore, L. (2001). *The limits of autobiography: Trauma and testimony.* Ithaca, NY and London: Cornell University Press.

Goldfield, D. (2002). *Still fighting the Civil War: The American South and southern history.* Baton Rouge: Louisiana State University Press.

Gray, R. (2000). *Southern aberrations: Writers of the American south and the problems of regionalism.* Baton Rouge: Louisiana State University Press.

Grosz, E. (1995). *Space, time, and perversion.* New York: Routledge.

Hackney, S. (2004). Identity politics, southern style. In A. Dunbar (Ed.), *Where we stand: Voices of southern dissent* (pp. 181–196). Montgomery, AL: New South Books.

Hale, G. E. (1998). *Making whiteness: The culture of segregation in the South, 1890–1940.* New York: Pantheon.

Harrison, R. P. (2002). Hic jacet. In W. J. T. Mitchell (Ed.), *Landscape and power* (second edition) (pp. 349–364). Chicago and London: University of Chicago Press.

Harrison, R. P. (2003). *The dominion of the dead.* Chicago: University of Chicago Press.

Harrison, S. (2003). Repudiating Faulkner: Race and responsibility in Ellen Douglas's *The Rock Cried Out. Southern Literary Journal,* 36(1), 1–20.

Henninger, K. R. (2004). How new? What place? Southern studies and the rest of the world. *Contemporary Literature,* 45(1), 177–186.

Hobson, F. (1991). *The southern writer in the postmodern world.* Athens and London: University of Georgia Press.

Hoggett, P., and Thompson, S. (2002). Toward a democracy of the emotions. *Constellations,* 9(1), 106–126.

Hooper, B. (2001). Desiring presence, romancing the real. *Annals of the Association of American Geographer,* 91(4), 703–716.

Jacobus, M. (1999). *Psychoanalysis and the scene of reading: The Clarendon lectures in English literature 1997.* Oxford: Oxford University Press.

Jones, S. W. (2002). I'll take my land: Contemporary southern agrarians. In S. W. Jones and S. Monteith (Eds.) *South to a new place: Region, literature, culture* (pp. 121–146). Baton Rouge: Louisiana State University Press.

Jones, S., and Monteith, S. (Eds.) (2002). *South to a new place: Region, literature, culture.* Baton Rouge: Louisiana State University Press.

Jordan, J. (2002). Report from the Bahamas. *Some of us did not die: New and selected essays of June Jordan* (pp. 211–222). New York: Basic Books.

Julie. (2001). Unpublished student paper. Course: Teaching, Schooling, and Society. Louisiana State University.

Kenan, R. (1992). Run, mourner, run. *Let the dead bury the dead:* Stories by Randall Kenan (pp. 163–191). San Diego, CA: Harcourt Brace & Company.

Kennedy, G. (1990). Place, self, and writing. *Southern Review.* 26 (3), 496–516.

Kincaid, J. (1990). Mariah. In S. Walker (Ed.), *The Graywolf annual seven: Stories from the American mosaic.* Saint Paul, MN : Graywolf Press.

Kincheloe, J. L., and Pinar, W. F. (1991). *Curriculum as social psychoanalysis: The significance of place.* Albany, NY: State University of New York Press.

Kincheloe, J. L., Pinar, W. F., and Slattery, P. (1994). A last dying chord? Toward cultural and educational renewal in the South. *Curriculum Inquiry*, 24(4), 407–437.

King, R. H. (1980). *A southern renaissance: The cultural awakening of the American south, 1930–1955.* Oxford: Oxford University Press.

Koeppel, B. (1999). Cancer alley, Louisiana. *Nation,* 269(15), 16–22.

Kolodny, A. (1975). *The lay of the land: Metaphor as experience and history in American life and letters.* Chapel Hill: University of North Carolina Press.

Komunyakaa, Y. (1992). *Magic city.* Hanover and London: University Press of New England.

Komunyakaa, Y. (2002a). Dark waters. In A. H. Deming and L. E. Savoy (Eds.), *The colors of nature: Culture, identity, and the natural world* (pp. 98–112). Minneapolis, MN: Milkweed Editions.

Komunyakaa, Y. (2002b). More than a state of mind. *Studies in the Literary Imagination.* 35(1), 163–164.

Komunyakaa, Y. (2003). Ignis fatuus. *New Republic,* 228(18), 32.

Kovel, J. (1984). *White racism.* London: Free Association Books.

Kreyling, M. (1998). *Inventing southern literature.* Jackson, MS: University Press of Mississippi.

LaCapra, D. (1997). Revisiting the historians' debate: Mourning and genocide. *History & Memory,* 9(1), 80–113.

Ladd, B. (2002). Dismantling the monolith: Southern places—past, present, and future. In S. W. Jones and S. Monteith (Eds.), *South to a new place: Region, literature, culture* (pp. 44–57). Baton Rouge: Louisiana State University Press.

Lane, C. (1998). The psychoanalysis and race: An introduction. In C. Lane (Ed.), *The psychoanalysis of race* (pp. 1–37). New York: Columbia University Press.

Laplanche J., and Pontalis J. -B. (1973). *The language of psycho-analysis* (D. Nicholson-Smith, Trans.). New York: W.W. Norton and Company.

Lewan, T., and Barclay, D. (2001). Torn from the land: Black Americans' farmland taken through cheating, intimidation, even murder. *Common Dreams* [On-line]. Available: http://www.commondreams.org/headlines01/1202-03.htm.

Lindsay. (2001). Unpublished student paper.

Lippard, L. R. (1997). *The lure of the local: Senses of place in a multicentered society.* New York: New Press.

Marriott, D. (1998). Bonding over phobia. In C. Lane (Ed.), *The psychoanalysis of race* (pp. 417–430). New York: Columbia University Press.

Massey, D. (1994). *Space, place, and gender.* Minneapolis, MN: University of Minnesota Press.

McKnight, R. (1998). The white boys. *White boys: Stories* (pp. 115–214). New York: Henry Holt and Company.

McPherson, T. (2003). *Reconstructing Dixie: Race, gender, and nostalgia in the imagined South.* Durham, NC, and London: Duke University Press.

Mitchell, W. J. T. (2002a). Preface to the second edition of *Landscape and Power:* Space, Place, and Landscape. In W. J. T. Mitchell (Ed.), *Landscape and power* (second edition) (pp. vii–xii). Chicago and London: University of Chicago Press.

Mitchell, W. J. T. (2002b). Introduction. In W. J. T. Mitchell (Ed.*),* *Landscape and power* (second edition) (pp. 1–4). Chicago and London: University of Chicago Press.

Mitchell, W. J. T. (2002c). Holy landscape: Israel, Palestine, and the American wilderness. In W. J. T. Mitchell (Ed.), *Landscape and power* (second edition) (pp. 26–290). Chicago and London: University of Chicago Press.

Moglen, S. (2005). On mourning social injury. *Psychoanalysis, culture, & society*, 10(2), 151–167.

Morris, M. (2001). *Curriculum and the Holocaust: Competing sites of memory and representation.* Mahwah, NJ: Lawrene Erlbaum Associates.

Morrison, T. (1992). *Playing in the dark: Whiteness and the literary imagination.* New York: Vintage Books.

Murphy, P. V. (2001). *The rebuke of history: The southern agrarians and American conservative thought.* Chapel Hill, NC: University of North Carolina Press.

Nora, P. (1989). Between memory and history: Les lieux de mémoire. *Representations,* 26(Spring), 7–25.

O'Brien, M. (1979). *The idea of the South: 1920–1941.* Baltimore and London: Johns Hopkins University Press.

Pinar, W. F. (1991). Curriculum as social psychoanalysis: On the significance of place. In J. L. Kincheloe and W. F. Pinar (Eds.), *Curriculum as social psychoanalysis: The significance of place* (pp. 165–186). Albany: State University of New York Press.

Pinar, W. F. (2001). *The Gender of racial politics and violence in America: Lynching, prison rape, & the crisis of masculinity.* New York: Peter Lang.

Pinar, W. F. (2004). *What is curriculum theory?* Mahwah, NJ: Lawrence Erlbaum Associates.

Pinar, W., and Grumet, M. (1976). *Toward a poor curriculum.* Dubuque, IA: Kendall/Hunt.

Pinar, W. F., Reynolds, W. M., Slattery, P., and Taubman, P. M. (1995). *Understanding curriculum: An introduction to historical and contemporary curriculum discourses.* New York: Peter Lang.

Pitt, A. (2003). *The play of the personal: Psychoanalytic narratives of feminist education.* New York: Peter Lang.

Ransom, J. C. (1930/1977). Reconstructed but unregenerate. In *I'll take my stand: The South and the agrarian tradition* (pp. 1–27). Baton Rouge and London: Louisiana State University Press.

Rich, A. (1976/1986). *Of woman born: Motherhood as experience and institution.* New York and London: W. W. Norton & Company.

Rich, A. (1984). Splittings. In *The fact of the doorframe: Poems selected and new, 1950–1984* (pp. 228–229). New York and London: W. W. Norton & Company.

Rich, A. (1991). An atlas of the difficult world. In *An atlas of the difficult world: Poems, 1988–1991* (pp. 3–26). New York and London: W. W. Norton & Company.

Richardson, M. (2002). *Being-in-Christ and putting death in its place: An anthropologist's account of Christian performance in Spanish America and the American South.* Baton Rouge: Louisiana State University Press.

Romine, S. (1999). *The narrative forms of southern community.* Baton Rouge: Louisiana State University Press.

Romine, S. (2002). Where is southern literature? The practice of place in a postmodern age. In S. W. Jones and S. Monteith (Eds.), *South to a new place: Region, literature, culture* (pp. 23–43). Baton Rouge: Louisiana State University Press.

Rubin, L. (1977). Introduction. In Twelve Southerners *I'll take my stand: The South and the agrarian tradition* (pp. xi–xxii). Baton Rouge and London: Louisiana State University Press.

Rubin, L. D., and Jacobs, R. D. (Eds.) (1953). *Southern renascence: The literature of the modern South.* Baltimore, MD: Johns Hopkins University Press.

Rustin, M. (1991). *The good society and the inner world.* London: Verso.

Salvio, P. (2001). Loss, memory and the work of learning: Lessons from the teaching life of Anne Sexton. In D. H. Holdstein and D. Bleich (Eds.), *Personal effects: The social character of scholarly writing* (pp. 93–117). Logan, UT: University of Utah Press.

Schreiber, E. J. (2001). *Subersive voices: Eroticizing the other in William Faulkner and Toni Morrison.* Knoxville: The University of Tennessee Press.

Sedgwick, E. K. (1985). *Between men: English literature and male homosocial desire.* New York: Columbia University Press

Silverman, K. (1992). *Male subjectivities at the margins.* New York and London: Routledge.

Silverman, K. (2000). *World spectators.* Stanford, CA: Stanford University Press.

Simon, R. I., Rosenberg. S., and Eppert, C. (Eds.) (2000). *Between hope & despair: Pedagogy and the remembrance of historical trauma.* Lanham, MD: Rowman & Littlefield Publishers, Inc.

Simpson, L. P. (1983). *The dispossessed garden.* Baton Rouge: Louisiana State University Press.

Slattery, P., and Daigle, K. (1994). Curriculum as a place of turmoil: Deconstructing the anguish in Walker Percy's Feliciana and Ernest Gaines' Point Coupee. *Curriculum Inquiry*, 24(4), 437–461.

Smith, G. J. (Ed.) (2003). *Agrarian letters: The correspondence of John Donald Wade and Donald Davidson, 1930–1939.* Macon, GA: Mercer University Press.

Smith, J. (2002). Southern culture on the skids: Punk, retro, narcissism, and the burden of *Southern history.* In S.W. Jones and S. Monteith (Eds.), *South to a new place: Region, literature, culture* (pp. 76–95). Baton Rouge: Louisiana State University Press.

Spirn, A. W. (1998). *The language of landscape.* New Haven, CT: Yale University Press.

Stevens, W. (1965). *The necessary angel: Essays on reality and the imagination.* New York: Vintage Books.

Styron, W. (1951/1992). *Lie down in darkness.* New York: Vintage International.

Twelve Southerners (1930/1977). *I'll take my stand. The South and the agrarian tradition.* Baton Rouge and London: Louisiana State University Press.

Wagner, J., and DiFeliciantonio, T. (Directors). (1997). *Girls like us* [Motion picture]. (Available from Women Make Movies, Inc., 462 Broadway, Suite 500WS New York, New York 10013).

Whitlock, R.U. (2007). *This corner of Canaan: Curriculum studies of place and the reconstruction of the South.* New York: Peter Lang.

Williams, R. (1977). *Marxism and literature.* New York: Oxford University Press.

Williamson, J. (1984). *The crucible of race: Black-white relations in the American South since emancipation.* New York and Oxford: Oxford University Press.

Winbush, R. A. (2003). And the earth moved: Stealing black land in the United States. In R. A. Winbush (Ed.), *Should America pay? Slavery and the raging debate on reparations.* (46–54). New York: HarperCollins.

Yaeger, P. (2000). *Dirt and desire: Reconstructing southern women's writing, 1930–1990.* Chicago and London: University of Chicago Press.

Zanes, W. (1998). Primitive myths: Photography and the American South. *Afterimage,* 25 (4), 10–12.

Žižek, S. (1989). *The sublime object of ideology.* London and New York: Verso.

Žižek, S. (1998). Love thy neighbor? No, thanks! In C. Lane (Ed.) *The Psychoanalysis of Race.* New York: Columbia University Press.

INDEX

C

D

E

F

G

Complicated Conversation

A BOOK SERIES OF CURRICULUM STUDIES

This series employs research completed in various disciplines to construct textbooks that will enable public school teachers to reoccupy a vacated public domain—not simply as "consumers" of knowledge, but as active participants in a "complicated conversation" that they themselves will lead. In drawing promiscuously but critically from various academic disciplines and from popular culture, this series will attempt to create a conceptual montage for the teacher who understands that positionality as aspiring to reconstruct a "public" space. *Complicated Conversation* works to resuscitate the progressive project—an educational project in which self-realization and democratization are inevitably intertwined; its task as the new century begins is nothing less than the intellectual formation of a public sphere in education.

The series editor is:

Dr. William F. Pinar
Department of Curriculum Studies
2125 Main Mall
Faculty of Education
University of British Columbia
Vancouver, British Columbia V6T 1Z4
CANADA

To order other books in this series, please contact our Customer Service Department:

(800) 770-LANG (within the U.S.)
(212) 647-7706 (outside the U.S.)
(212) 647-7707 FAX

Or browse online by series:

www.peterlang.com